Profiles of America

CHICAGO
IN COLOR

Profiles of America

CHICAGO
in Color

A Collection of Color Photographs by
ARCHIE LIEBERMAN

With an Introductory Text and Notes on the Illustrations by
ROBERT CROMIE

HASTINGS HOUSE · PUBLISHERS
New York, 10016

PUBLISHED 1969 BY HASTINGS HOUSE, PUBLISHERS, INC.
Reprinted February 1976
All rights reserved, including the right to reproduce
this book or portions thereof in any form or by any means,
electronic or mechanical, including photocopying,
recording or by any information storage and retrieval system,
without permission in writing from the publishers.

Published simultaneously in Canada by
Saunders, of Toronto, Ltd., Don Mills, Ontario

Library of Congress Catalog Card Number: 75-78251
ISBN Number: 8038-1203-5

Printed and bound in Hong Kong by Mandarin Publishers Limited

CONTENTS

CONTENTS

Chicago: The Past is Prologue   11

THE PLATES

The John Hancock—Chicago's Tallest	33
The Skyline off Lake Michigan	35
Piper's Alley, a Segment of Old Town	37
The Water Tower, Relic of the Chicago Fire	39
The Twins of Marina City	41
The Big Clocks at Marshall Field's	43
The Chicago Free Fair	45
The Picnic That Ties Up the Town	47
State Street, the Shoppers' Mecca	49
The Shrine of St. Jude Thaddeus	51
Oriental Custom With a Western Slant	53
The Art Institute and Its Guardians	55
The Longest Fresh-water Race	57
Fish of Every Shape and Color	59
Traffic on the Ike	61
A Haven for Budding Lawyers	63
The Campus at Chicago Circle	65
A Promenade Up the Avenue	67
Where the Naval Recruits Come From	69
Rockefeller Chapel and Its Bells	71
Plants for Beauty and for Use	73
Beasts and Games for the Millions	75
As Pure a Product as Spring Water	77

A Way to Explore the Heavens	79
Down in a Coal Mine	81
Landmarks in the Loop	83
Why and Wherefore of the Loop	85
Arrivals at Busy O'Hare Airport	87
The Ever-Changing Skyline	89
Why an Air View is Superior	91
Picasso's Talk of the Town	93
Ready for a Summer Sail	95

CHICAGO: THE PAST IS PROLOGUE

Chicago: The Past is Prologue

I

EVERY TOWN worth bothering about has some quality that is unique, some set of memories that contributes to its personality.

London's fascination, I suspect, is compounded of the lingering presence of Dr. Sam Johnson, Winston Churchill, Charles Dickens, Sherlock Holmes (still alive, I am told, and raising bees on the Sussex Downs), Shakespeare, and a host of others, including any number of beautiful women, both chaste and wanton. Then there are Fleet Street, Tower Bridge, the Thames, Big Ben, St. Paul's, the little theater beneath the Savoy Hotel, Hyde Park, the ghost of Ranelagh Gardens, and hundreds of bits and pieces from many centuries.

Paris? The Seine, of course, and the exhilarating sound of a foreign language. The Left Bank, Notre Dame Cathedral, the Arc de Triomphe, trees, lights, open-air cafés, and the Folies Bergère. Cyrano, naturally, and the Three Musketeers, the Eiffel Tower, the Bastille, the day the Nazis were driven out, Josephine Baker . . .

Los Angeles, to my mind, resembles a movie set, and I have always thought that the Angelenos might wake up some morning to find the whole town being dismantled and hauled away.

San Francisco, on the other hand, and New Orleans, possess an authentic magic of their own: cable cars, Chinatown, Fisherman's Wharf, the Top of the Mark, Rampart and Bourbon Streets, the Mardi Gras, Paul Morphy, the chess master; Lafcadio Hearne, Louis Armstrong, Pirate's Alley . . .

Chicago, incorporated as a town in 1833 and a city four years later, has as its civic motto the phrase: *I Will,* and a restlessness of spirit to go with it. This particular characteristic long has been noted by observers of the Chicago scene.

"Chicago, Chicago, that toddlin' town . . ." wrote Fred Fisher in 1922, and the description was apt.

Carl Sandburg, poet and Lincoln biographer, described it in 1916 as, "Stormy, husky, brawling, City of the Big Shoulders." And a later chronicler, Nelson Algren, who still makes Chicago his starting-out point—he was on assignment in South Vietnam as this was written—caught the same feeling in more contemporary terms when he entitled a 1951 book, *Chicago, City on the Make.*

Chicago is filled with motion. Lake Michigan prowls ceaselessly on its eastern threshold and sometimes, on wintry days, slashes across the Outer Drive and makes that thoroughfare impassable. It is a rare sight to see the waters in a placid mood; a common thing to hear, in the middle of a weather announcement, that storm warnings are up for small craft on the lake.

Rail traffic, which glides in from the east, west, north, and south, has established Chicago as one of the world's greatest freight centers. Some of the crack passenger trains have vanished: the Twentieth Century Limited, most glamorous of them all in days gone by, from which Bob Elson used to conduct celebrity interviews over the radio; the Twin Cities 400, which used to head up through Wisconsin and Minnesota; the Illinois Central's Green Diamond, and the beautifully-named Phoebe Snow. But others still run on schedule: Santa Fe's Super-Chief and San Francisco Chief, the California and Denver Zephyrs, the Broadway Limited, Capitol Limited and Panama Limited, the Blue Bird, the Empire Builder, the morning and evening Hiawathas, and other proud standard bearers.

The amount of lake shipping is not what it was, so far as Chicago is concerned, although paper carriers from Canada still bring newsprint to the city's four major dailies, and occasional freighters heading into the Chicago River force street traffic to halt as the bridges swing into the air, one after another.

But Chicago has been a world port since 1959, when the St. Lawrence Seaway was opened, and freighters from half a hundred lines, flying foreign flags, appear regularly in Chicago and depart for dozens of strange ports. Many of these ocean-going ships offer accommodations for a few passengers, and bring visitors to town or take Chicagoans overseas.

Near the Planetarium and Aquarium, on Northerly Island, Meigs Field, a postage-stamp airdrome compared with O'Hare, accommodates small executive planes, commuter airlines and helicopters, and is very busy indeed.

To the west, on the other edge of town, are the resurgent Midway, once Chicago's biggest airport, which again handles commercial traffic, and the forever frenzied O'Hare Field, named in memory of Lieutenant-Commander Edward (Butch) O'Hare, one of the heroes of South Pacific fighting, who posthumously won the Medal of Honor. O'Hare is a great airport from which you can take off for anywhere on earth almost any hour of the day or night on a dozen domestic lines, or an equal number of international ones. You will find O'Hare immortalized as Lincoln International, in Arthur Hailey's best-selling novel *Airport*.

Needless to say, buses and trucks rumble in and out of Chicago on good roads at an incredible rate, and if you want to drive your own car, you can reach Davenport, Iowa, 180 miles away, in less than three hours without any sense of having hurried, while it is possible to pick up one of the Chicago expressways and drive east to New York City without interference from a single traffic light en route.

II

CHICAGO, TOO, is a city of memories. Abraham Lincoln was nominated for the Presidency in the Wigwam on May 18, 1860, and the Great Chicago Fire of 1871 left ninety thousand homeless and destroyed almost the whole town. Although there is no proof whatever to support the story that the blaze began when one of Mrs. O'Leary's cows kicked over a lantern in her barn on DeKoven Street, the legend dies hard.

If it seems unbelievable that so small a beginning could mushroom into a blazing inferno from which burning brands even threatened a water intake crib two miles out in the lake, remember that the city was parched from lack of rain, that its houses, fences, stores, and even sidewalks were made of wood; that the Fire Department was worn out fighting big and little fires for more than thirty-six hours, and that a monstrous wind carried the flames from one rooftop to another, firing the masts of the ships as it crossed the river, and igniting the Waterworks on the North Side as well.

It is on record that Matthias Benner, an assistant fire marshal, came out of a building near the O'Leary cottage, not too long after the alarm was sounded, convinced that the conflagration was under control, only to be told by John Schank, the first assistant marshal, to send all available equipment north.

"John," asked the startled Benner, "where has the fire gone to?"

"To hell and gone," Schank replied with admirable accuracy.

If you would like a picture of Chicago just before the Great Fire, and will make allowances for the sardonic humor of one of the town's newspapermen, Franc B. Wilkie, you could do worse than read his *Walks About Chicago*, published in 1869.

He says, for example, speaking of the West Side:

"There are no carriages in Westside. It is so dusty there that a vehicle which does not run on rails can never find its way from one point to another. When it is not dusty it is muddy. The dust has no top and the mud no bottom. In either case, locomotion, except on tracks, is impossible.

"Westside has no newspapers. It likewise has no opera-house which is used as a circus. Its principal amusement consists, among the men, in chewing tobacco, and among the women, in going to church. Wherever there is a corner in Westside not occupied as a drug store, it is occupied by a church . . .

"There is one church, on the corner of Washington avenue and Robey avenue, that has been tolling its bell without cessation for two years. When there isn't a prayer-meeting, or some body dead, they toll it for some body who is going to die. They use up a sexton there every thirteen days. When there is no prayer-meeting, or any thing else, or any body dead, or any body who is going to die, then the bell tolls for the last deceased sexton."

Commenting on the newly-opened water tunnel, which provided Chicago with clean, pure water for the first time in its history. Wilkie said:

"The cleansing properties of the new water are wonderful. Children whose faces have been washed in it have been lost and never found. Their mothers can not recognize them. It is proposed to establish a place where lost children may be gathered, and where only the old water will be used in their ablutions. In time, it is expected that many young children, whom nobody now knows, will be recognized by their parents.

"Long-married people who wash themselves in the new water undergo all the satisfaction of a newly-married pair. She seems some other woman. He appears some other man. The jaded routine of their old life disappears. There are the freshness, the piquancy, of a new love. She is tender, believing him some gentle stranger. He is gallant, thinking her some beautiful young Thing . . ."

At the time Wilkie was writing, Chicago's population was close to 300,000—an astronomical increase over the 4,170 of 1837, when town became city. And even this figure, to keep dropping backward in time, would hardly have been believed in 1812 when it was decided to evacuate Fort Dearborn for fear of attack by the British or their Indian allies.

General William Hull, who commanded the United States forces in the area, decided to order the abandonment of Fort Dearborn "provided it can be effected with a greater prospect of safety than to remain." Somehow this "provided" clause was omitted from the directive received by Captain Nathan Heald, commanding the fort, and against the warnings of Black Partridge, a friendly Potawatomi chief, Heald and about one hundred others, including soldiers and settlers, on August 15, 1812, started out for Fort Wayne.

They were barely two miles from their starting point when they were ambushed by an Indian war party and about half of them killed. All of the survivors, except the John Kinzie family whom the Indians liked, were taken prisoner and held for ransom. The fort was put to the torch the next day and not rebuilt until 1816.

Chicago never has been a stranger to violence and disaster. In the spring of 1886, during a period of labor unrest, seven policemen were killed when someone tossed a bomb into a mass meeting held to protest the fatal shooting of seven strikers by police. The meeting, it is generally agreed, was peaceably conducted and probably would have broken up quietly if an excitable police inspector had not ordered his men to break it up by force.

Even though no one ever found out who hurled the bomb, eight socalled "anarchists" were arrested and tried. Seven received death sentences, and of those four were hanged and one killed himself. The other two had their sentences commuted to life imprisonment, and the eighth man was given a fifteen-year term.

Governor John Peter Altgeld, whose life story has been superbly told in *Eagle Forgotten*, by Harry Barnard, Chicago author and teacher, later threw away his political career by pardoning the three remaining Haymarket "rioters" because he believed them innocent. Altgeld also issued a scathing indictment of the conduct of the trial judge, Joseph E. Gary.

The Haymarket affair was followed by the strife-studded Pullman strike of 1894, for which Eugene Debs and three other American Railway Union officials served six months for contempt of court, a sentence whose comparative mildness was a tribute to the union's defense attorney, Clarence Darrow. By this time Chicago had a population in excess of one million, and Jane Addams, a pioneer social worker, was operating Hull House as a neighborhood center.

Costly as was the Great Chicago Fire in terms of property, fewer than 200 bodies were recovered, and two other disasters followed in which the human toll was far greater. On December 30, 1903, 571 persons died when the Iroquois Theater caught fire during a holiday matinee, and more than 800 were drowned on July 24, 1915, when the excursion steamer *Eastland*, with an overload of passengers aboard, capsized at her Clark Street pier.

There has been a vast amount of gang violence, too, over the years. While Alphonse (Scarface Al) Capone, who rose to prominence during Prohibition days, managed to die a natural if unsavory death, other big-name gangsters were less fortunate. In fact more than a thousand Chicagoans of dubious reputation made noisy exits during this more or less private war, among them Dion O'Banion, who was gunned down in his flower shop across the street from Holy Name Cathedral in the autumn of 1924; Hymie Weiss, killed from ambush in the same neighborhood; Big Jim Colosimo, one of the first to go, who was shot in his own restaurant, and of course six of the seven—one merely a hanger-on—who died on St. Valentine's Day, 1929, riddled by machinegun fire in a North Clark Street garage by five executioners, three of them disguised as policemen.

Among the seven on that still-echoing occasion was one Frank Gusenberg, who fought for life long enough for the police to ask who shot him. Gusenberg was true to the gangster code.

"Nobody shot me," he said, and died a short time later.

O'Banion, it might be added, while originally buried in unconsecrated ground, was reburied by his widow in consecrated ground in Mount Carmel cemetery at a later date. This drew from Captain John Stege of the Chicago police force this wry comment:

"O'Banion was a thief and a murderer, but look at him now, buried eighty feet from a bishop."

There have been other murderous outbursts with no gangland motivation. The Suzanne Degnan case, for which William Heirens still serves time in Stateville; the senseless slaughter of eight student nurses in 1967 by Richard Speck; various multiple killings for which no solution was ever found and—perhaps most talked-about of all—the horrible and casual killing in 1924 of little Bobby Franks. Nathan Leopold, one of the two murderers, was pardoned some thirty years later after his partner in crime, Richard Loeb, had died in prison. Clarence Darrow appeared for the defense in the Franks case, too.

There is a temptation, perhaps because of Chicago's reputation for violence, to linger within mental earshot of the gunfire. Eddie Waitkus, a pretty good first baseman for the Philadelphia Phillies, and before them the Cubs, was shot and wounded by a highly-strung young woman in the Edgwater Beach hotel in 1949. The lady with the pistol, a stranger to the ballplayer, had admired him from afar and chose this odd method of expressing her regard.

And there was John Dillinger, the Indian farm boy turned bank robber, who was betrayed by the Lady in Red and killed by FBI agents in an alley near the Biograph Theater on North Lincoln Avenue in 1934, ending a long and frustrating chase.

Before this, in 1920 to be exact, Carl Wanderer was briefly a hero, following the deaths of his pregnant wife and an unidentified and shabbily-dressed man, when Wanderer explained that he had managed to kill the man only after the fellow had shot Mrs. Wanderer during a holdup attempt.

When both guns were traced to Wanderer, however, he was asked to run through his story again, and this time admitted that he had hired the "holdup man" as part of a madly bungled scheme to get rid of his wife. Wanderer had paid the dupe, who quickly became known in news stories as the Ragged Stranger, to fake a robbery attempt so that Wanderer could drive him away and play the role of hero. But when the stranger showed up, Wanderer calmly killed both his wife and the man he had tricked.

The Ragged Stranger, still nameless, was buried through the charity of a Chicago restaurant man, and the whole curious incident is now largely forgotten. As recently as 1952, however, the late Charles Collins of the *Chicago Tribune*, in a story of the crime, created this enviable paragraph as he described Wanderer and his wife returning home on their final evening together, just before confrontation with the stranger:

"They walked slowly, because Mrs. Wanderer was heavy with child—and her husband was heavy with guns."

III

CHICAGO'S MAYORS often have been colorful. Long John Wentworth, who is said to have arrived barefoot in town in 1836, went on to become a newspaper editor, mayor, congressman, and the city's largest landowner, and personally in 1859 led a raid that resulted in the destruction of an area called The Sands, where dwelt certain ladies of what used to be known as "ill-repute". Wentworth, after whom one of the horse-drawn engines used during the Chicago Fire was named, is said to have been 6 feet 6 inches tall and to have weighed 300 pounds. His eighteen-room farmhouse, built in 1868 and recently torn down, had ceilings 12 feet high and doors 8 feet in height.

Years after Long John's foray against the women of The Sands, two sisters of similar stamp but with far more luxurious quarters opened the Everleigh Club near 22nd Street, a brothel so decorously run that it drew as customers a great many of Chicago's better citizens and became internationally known. It was its fame in fact, which doomed the club. Mayor Carter Harrison ordered it closed, so the story goes, when someone showed him a pamphlet in which the Stockyards and the Everleigh Club both were listed as sights no visitor to Chicago should miss. This was in 1911, and Harrison's order prevailed despite objections from First Ward politicians and police officials.

You will find a variety of information about Minna and Ada Everleigh, and their club, in the files of the Chicago Historical Society, which is on Clark Street just above North Avenue, a short cab ride from downtown. The society is an unbelievably complete repository of mementoes from yesterday. These include portraits, maps, books, manuscripts, diaries, furniture, vehicles, and even Abraham Lincoln's top hat and the table on which Robert E. Lee signed the surrender papers tendered by Ulysses S. Grant.

It is not easily available, but Moran's *Dictionary of Chicago*, "an alphabetically arranged dictionary, comprising all of the interests that contribute to Chicago's greatness," does manage to convey a sense of what the city was like in other years. Here, to tempt you into tracking down a copy of Moran's, are some excerpts from the 1909 edition:

"***Automobiles***—There are over 6,000 licensed automobiles in Chicago . . . It seems as if the horse is doomed to be supplanted by the horseless carriage . . ."

"***Billiards***—Amateurs of this game, who are strangers in Chicago, would do well to remember that billiard sharps, as well as billiard tables, abound in every quarter of the city, and should therefore be wary of nice young men who want to bet a trifle on the game. Whenever this is done the stranger's game is apt to improve marvelously at critical moments."

"***Fortune in Lost Articles***—If a man could find everything that is lost in Chicago for a whole month he need do nothing for the rest of his life but make faces at the banks . . ."

"***Free Public Baths***—During the year 1908, the fourteen public baths have been well patronized, showing an increase over the number of baths given in the preceding year . . .

"Total number bathed: 865,834. Average cost each bath given, 6.1 cents."

*"**Immoral Pictures**—Much satisfaction is felt by the members of the theater censoring squad over the decision handed down recently by the Supreme Court upholding the right of the city to exercise police power in censoring immoral pictures."*

Three other mayors also have added considerably to the city's fame. There was Mayor William Hale (Big Bill) Thompson (1915–23 and 1927–31), a dedicated Anglophobe, whose principal object of hatred was King George III (1760–1820). Also Mayor Anton (Tony) Cermak, who was fatally wounded in 1933 in Miami by an assassin's bullet intended for Franklin Delano Roosevelt and said only: "I'm glad it was me instead of you." And Mayor Richard J. Daley, head of one of the most powerful Democratic machines ever put together, who was one of the nation's most talked-about figures as a result of the televised people vs. police confrontation during the 1968 Democratic Convention.

Little Egypt was the sex symbol at the World's Columbian Exposition of 1893, although not described in exactly those terms, and Sally Rand made the fan famous during the World's Fair of 1933. John Dillinger, while on the lam, paid an unobtrusive visit to that fair, posing for a photograph with an unsuspecting policeman. And a young golfer, Joe Jemsek, who now runs four public courses in the Chicago area, used to amaze fair patrons by the great distances he could drive golf balls out over the lake.

It might be worth quoting Theodore Dreiser here on his reaction to the World's Columbian Exposition, a reaction shared by many who could not express it quite so well:

"All at once and out of nothing, in this dingy city of six or seven hundred thousand, which but a few years before had been a wilderness of wet grass and mud flats, and by this lake, which but a hundred years before was a lone silent waste, had now been reared this vast and harmonious collection of perfectly constructed and showy buildings, containing in their delightful interiors, the artistic, mechanical and scientific achievements of the world." Chicago in 1893 had more than eleven hundred thousand residents. The Fair and the nineteenth century's worst depression coincided. Twenty-four Chicago banks failed during the first eight months of 1893, and unemployment soared to desperate heights, but the Exposition was a huge success.

IV

CHICAGO ALWAYS HAS been known as a good sports town. The "long count" fight between Jack Dempsey and Gene Tunney, won by Tunney, a decision still argued fiercely by fight fans, was held in Soldier Field in 1927, with more than one hundred thousand paying a record $2,600,000 for the privilege of saying, "I was there!" Virtually every other great boxer of the last half century also has been seen in a Chicago ring.

Joe Louis, who first appeared as a Golden Glover out of Detroit; Sugar Ray Robinson, a dancer dangerous as a lightning flash, who may indeed be the best, pound for pound, who ever stepped into the ring; Tony Zale and Rocky Graziano, one of whose three savage title fights drew a capacity throng to the Chicago Stadium (Zale won this on a sixth round kayo in 1947); Ezzard Charles, the gentleman from Cincinnati; nifty Johnny Bratton, whose luck finally turned bad; Jersey Joe Walcott, Rocky Marciano, Kid Gavilan and his much advertised "bolo" punch.

Add the names of Mohammad Ali (Cassius Clay); Sonny Liston, who came snarling to meet Ali and was quickly tamed; Floyd Patterson, whose hobby was reading the dictionary; Archie Moore, who threatened to go on forever, and a swinging host of others, among them Kingfish Levinsky, who will live in ring history for one of the best explanations ever given of why a fighter was so quickly kayoed by the hard-hitting Louis.

"I must have been in a transom," said the King.

There were the Chicago Black Sox, switching to baseball, so named because some of them threw the 1919 World Series, but they are more than counter-balanced by a crowd of other baseball immortals such as Frank Chance of Tinker-to-Evers-to-Chance fame; Eddie Walsh, Ray Schalk, the fabled Dizzy Dean, in his final years a hurler; Luke (Old Aches and Pains) Appling, who played his best when complaining the most; and of course Ernie Banks, Pride of the Cubs. Add the graceful Luis Aparicio, the indomitable Minnie Minoso, who crowded the plate the first time he batted after recovering from a skull fractured by a pitch; Billy Pierce, a southpaw of great distinction and even, in the twilight of one of the longest and most glittering careers of any athlete, the crafty Leroy (Satchel) Paige, who was of major league caliber long before he finally got his chance at the big time through the color-blind Bill Veeck. Paige is remembered for his superb control and pitching skill, and also for his advice on how to live:

"Don't look back. Something might be gaining on you."

George Herman (Babe) Ruth, during the 1932 World Series, drove a ball into the center-field seats in Wrigley Field and created a facet of baseball history which still is hotly disputed.

Did the flamboyant Babe actually point a finger at the spot where he intended to send the next pitch? There are those who will swear that he did, but I prefer to trust the word of Leo (Gabby) Hartnett, Cubs catcher, who was closer to Ruth than anyone when the controversial incident took place. In an interview years later Hartnett said:

"He came up in the fifth inning and took two called strikes. After each one, the Cub bench gave him the business—stuff like he was choking up and washed up.

"Then Babe waved his hand across the plate toward the Cub bench on the third base side. One finger was up. At the same time he said softly—I think only the umpire and myself heard him—'It takes only one to hit it!'

"Charles Root then came in with a fast ball and bam, it went into the center field seats.

"In that 1932 series, we tried every kind of pitch on him. It didn't make any difference. He rammed the ball down our throats. There'll never be another like him."

The temptation, as a former sportswriter, is to continue: George (Papa Bear) Halas and his great teams. The Cardinals. The ill-fated Rockets and Hornets. Red Grange, the galloping ghost. Gale Sayers, one of the most exciting runners of all time. Paul Christman, quarterback-turned-announcer, and Lou Boudreau, shortstop-turned-announcer, both of whom started a trend that still continues. There are dozens more, which it would be unfair to name unless the list were complete.

Two of the world's bestknown athletes were and are Chicagoans. Charles (Chick) Evans, who won virtually every golfing title worth having and needed only seven clubs to take the National Open crown, is perhaps proudest of having founded the Evans' Scholars Foundation, which provides money to send caddies to college. Jesse Owens turned the 1936 Olympic Games in Berlin into a lovely rebuttal of the Hitler theory on Aryan supremacy.

Let us, again for reasons of space, skip lightly over such unfading pictures as the wedge shot at the eighteenth hole at Tam O'Shanter, which ran in for a deuce to give Lew Worsham the 1953 World title just as Chandler Harper seemed to have the top prize of $50,000 all wrapped up. Or the 1949 National Open tourney at Medinah's No. 3 course, won by Cary Middlecoff over a layout that frustrated the touring professionals so thoroughly that Charles Einstein, then a Chicago sportswriter, was moved to remark that Medinah, with its unyielding rough and beckoning trees, "resembles the place where the elephants go to die."

V

IT SHOULD BE remembered, sports fans, that Chicago is a city of culture as well as brawn. She has superb libraries, among them the Newberry, where scholars go for source material in such fields as Americana, literature, and music; the John Crerar, a research institution specializing in science and technology, and the collection of the Chicago Historical Society, whose Chicago material includes the handwritten report of the formal inquiry into the great fire.

The Newberry, while it offers public exhibitions and sells its own publications, is primarily for working purposes, and its wealth of material, which is literally priceless, is far too large to attempt a catalogue here. But if you can prove the need for it, you can examine a folio Shakespeare or some of the rarer items of incunabula or enough other scarce-as-a-unicorn items to keep you busy for decades.

Jory Graham, in her new *Chicago Guide*, lists this pleasantly macabre information about Walter Loomis Newberry, the nineteenth-century Chicagoan who endowed the Library:

"His death was rather strange; it occurred on a European-bound liner, and the captain, instead of burying him at sea, placed his body in a cask of Medford rum that was part of the cargo and eventually returned cask and corpse to Chicago for burial in Graceland Cemetery."

Then there is the Chicago Public Library, one of the major institutions of the country, stocking more than three million books and enjoying an annual circulation of more than ten million. It still preserves a collection donated by Queen Victoria to help replace books destroyed in the Great Fire.

Universities and colleges proliferate in Chicago and environs. The University of Chicago, with an endowment approaching three hundred million dollars, had international stature even before it produced the first nuclear chain reaction in 1942. Northwestern University, based in nearby Evanston, the only privately endowed member of the Big Ten, reaches into Chicago at the McKinlock Campus on the North Side. Roosevelt University, dating only from 1945, inhabits the famous Auditorium Building on the Lake Front. The University of Illinois, at home in Urbana, flourishes also on its Circle Campus in Chicago.

Institutions dealing with every form of the humanities, science, and the arts, include such familiar names as the Illinois Institute of Technology, DePaul, Loyola, Columbia—which trains students for journalism and the communications media—Mundelein and a number of others in the suburbs, among them Wheaton and Lake Forest.

Many of the nation's top authors rose to fame after an apprenticeship as newspapermen in Chicago. Carl Sandburg reported labor activities and at least one race riot; the house in which he composed *Chicago Poems* still stands at 4646 Hermitage Avenue, but efforts to make it a literary shrine have come to naught. Eugene Field, who conducted a column, *Sharps and Flats*, in the *Chicago Daily News* from 1883 to his death in 1895, will always be known, I suspect and believe, for his *Little Boy Blue* and the poem about Wynken, Blynken, and Nod. Field is buried at the Church of the Holy Comforter in Kenilworth, a northern suburb.

George Ade collaborated with John T. McCutcheon in *Stories of the Streets and of the Town* before *The College Widow* and other plays made him wealthy, and Ring Lardner garnered the stories in *You Know Me, Al* while touring with baseball teams for the *Chicago Tribune*. Westbrook Pegler wrote some of his best copy while on the same staff, and after inditing a powerful but restrained appeal to sentiment he closed with: "Someone told me I couldn't turn it on, and I said the hell I couldn't." Ben Hecht and Charles MacArthur drew on their former associates when writing the most famous of all newspaper comedies, *The Front Page*. MacArthur married Helen Hayes after a courtship begun when he offered her a bag of peanuts at their first meeting, saying, "I wish they were emeralds."

The stimulation of news reporting continues. Vincent Starrett is a veteran now; his *The Private Life of Sherlock Holmes* is a first-edition rarity; with Christopher Morley he founded the Baker Street Irregulars, uniting Sherlockian enthusiasts all over the world. But Meyer Levin is still active as he divides his time between the United States and Israel; Chicago inspired *The Old Bunch* and *Compulsion*, the latter based on a notorious murder case. Active, too, are Lloyd Wendt and Herman Kogan, collaborators on several timely books, including *Lords of the Levee* about Chicago's seamy political life; Bill Mauldin, cartoonist of the *Sun-Times*, who also writes books; Claudia Cassidy, former drama critic of the *Tribune*, and Hoke Norris, Mike Royko and Van Allen Bradley of the *Daily News*.

Sherwood Anderson dreamed up *Winesburg, Ohio* while writing advertising copy in Chicago; Theodore Dreiser imagined the heroine of *Sister Carrie* haunting West Van Buren Street; Frank Norris, who pioneered in naturalism in *McTeague*, drew on a crisis in the Chicago grain market for *The Pit*. Born a Chicagoan, he was dead at thirty-two. Willard Motley's *Knock on Any Door* was a powerful story of the Chicago slums; he died in Mexico in 1966. Jack Conroy, author of *The Disinherited*, one of the early proletarian novels, lived in Chicago until he retired to his home town, Moberly, Missouri, in the mid-sixties. Other living authors who demand attention include Gwendolyn Brooks, the only black writer to win a Pulitzer prize—with *Annie Allen* in 1950. She came to Chicago from her native Kansas at an early age and is now Poet Laureate of Illinois. Also active in literary circles is Saul Bellow, winner of National Book Awards with *The Adventures of Augie March* and *Herzog*, a member of the faculty at the University of Chicago.

Most influential—at least on literary style—was Ernest Hemingway, who lived in his formative years in suburban Oak Park, but developed his writing remote from Chicago and rarely is included in the Chicago galaxy. If there are echoes of his youthful experiences in the novels that brought him fame, they are not discernible. Quite the opposite, however, is the work of James T. Farrell, whose famous character, Studs Lonigan, was the first in a long procession of young people who live on Chicago's South Side. Author of more than forty novels, Farrell now makes his home in New York.

Lloyd Lewis, former sports editor and drama critic for the *Chicago Daily News*, was a Civil War buff and wrote a biography of General W. T. Sherman and *Myths After Lincoln* long before the war became popular reading. Dying at fifty-seven in 1949, he did not live to complete his ambitious life of Grant, of which only the first volume, *Captain Sam Grant*, was published. The biography was finished by Bruce Catton.

One of the best-known of living Chicago authors is Nelson Algren, who won the National Book Award for *The Man with the Golden Arm*, and is little affected by his fame. A clue to the Algren character came a couple of years ago when Chicago police stopped a car containing Algren and a couple of friends and found therein a single marijuana cigarette. Algren was recognized and told he could leave. He refused to do so.

"If you book them," he said coldly, "book me too. When I'm with a guy I'm with a guy."

The case later was dismissed.

Richard Wright (1909–60), came to Chicago from the south when he was nine, and with the appearance of *Native Son* in 1940, became recognized as one of the nation's powerful novelists. He died an expatriate in Paris a few years ago. Louis (Studs) Terkel who wrote the best-selling *Division Street: America*, is an expert on jazz, folk music, and baseball; Harry Mark Petrakis, son of a Greek Orthodox priest, has done several novels about our Greek-American community, including *A Dream of Kings*, which was made into a movie with Anthony Quinn as Matsoukas.

Not to be overlooked are Paul Angle, former director of the Chicago Historical Society, a Lincoln scholar and writer; Prof. William H. McNeill, who won the National Book Award for history with *The Rise and Fall of the West*; Prof. John Hope Franklin, another of the University of Chicago's top historians; Lerone Bennett, whose *Before the Mayflower*, gave sharp impetus to greater attention to black history, and Mary Jane Ward, whose title, *The Snake Pit*, has become part of the language.

Others include Prof. Clarence ver Steeg of the Northwestern University history faculty; Prof. Ernest Samuels of Northwestern, who won a Pulitzer prize for his study of Henry Adams; Prof. Bergen Evans, the word sleuth, whose book of quotations is a sturdy rival to Bartlett's; and Prof. Richard Stern, novelist and short story writer from the Midway.

Many nationally-famous publications have had their origin in Chicago. This is the home port of that huge compendium of information, the *Encyclopaedia Britannica*. Here appears *Who's Who in America* and its related publications. Here are the headquarters of John Johnson's thriving *Ebony* magazine, and Heffner's *Playboy* and the cavorting bunnies. Here, remote from entertainment but deep in culture is *Poetry, A Magazine of Verse*, founded more than half a century ago by Harriet Monroe and still opening the gates to poets. As for printing national publications, Chicago deals only in tonnage. Millions of copies of magazines and telephone directories issue from presses that run night and day.

Chicago is well served by large daily newspapers, which include the *Tribune*, the *Sun-Times* and the *Daily News*. It has many radio stations and enough television channels to offer a wide choice for the careful viewer, among them Channel 11, which is affiliated with the National Educational network and often takes chances with the views it airs, a circumstance that sometimes sets the WTTW switchboard aglow and makes Edward Morris, director of programming, wish he were once again living the quiet life of a demolition expert in World War II.

Ralph G. Newman's Abraham Lincoln Bookshop on Chestnut Street is a treasure chest of Americana. Its life-size figure of Old Abe was so imposing that even Newman would be startled when he entered the shop at night.

Visitors, gazing up at the tall frame of the John Hancock Building, should reflect that in Chicago rose the first steel skyscraper. Daniel Burnham, Dankmar Adler, and Louis Sullivan left their impress on the city's commercial buildings, but Frank Lloyd Wright developed the prairie style of dwellings all around Chicago, and his Robie House is considered one of his best creations. Here came Mies Van der Rohe and other great ones, and here Lorado Taft embellished the city with his sculpture.

For many years Chicagoans kept looking wistfully toward New York, and some of those who didn't pull out for Manhatten developed a kind of civic inferiority complex, which was not lessened when A. J. Liebling, a carpetbagger from the east, wrote a study called *The Second City*. Chicagoans treated visiting New Yorkers as if they came from a superior planet. But this attitude has changed and even New Yorkers say, cautiously, that they would not mind living here. A prominent author asked if I would be surprised if he and his wife, a former actress and a glamorous redhead, moved here from New York. I assured him I would not.

For Chicago is conscious of certain advantages. It has not been without lights since 1871. It has not had a water shortage such as periodically hits New York, nor a garbage collectors' or major teachers' strike. And unless a really heavy snowstorm falls, it is relatively free from massive traffic jams.

Chicago's Art Institute stands preeminent, and the great Chicago Symphony Orchestra has led in musical culture for generations. Well-stocked bookstores supply the reading wants of a huge region. And the winds that blow off Lake Michigan give the citizens the feeling that they are able to breathe. As a metropolis surrounded by golf courses, Chicago is one of the few cities in which it is possible to tee off on a Saturday or Sunday morning without first obtaining a court order.

THE PLATES

THE JOHN HANCOCK—CHICAGO'S TALLEST

Anyone looking southeast towards the lake from this leafy vantage point in Lincoln Park finds the view usurped by the hundred-story John Hancock Building, which towers 1,107 feet above the rush and roar of upper Michigan Avenue traffic. The tallest office-and-apartment structure in the world, which, with a kind of inverted snobbery, was halted only 16 feet below the record height of New York City's Empire State Building, is corseted against the buffeting winds by great steel cross-pieces (five on each side) as well as by its tapering form, which narrows from 50,000 square feet at ground level to 16,000 at the top. Twin television antennas 349 feet high give added grace.

Ground was broken for Big John—as a *Chicago Daily News* reporter nicknamed it—on May 4, 1965, and the skeleton work was topped off three years and two days later. There is enough steel in the Hancock's framework to construct 28,000 automobiles, and 11,459 panes of glass allow the sun easy access. The neighborly courtesy of the Playboy Building to the north, as exemplified by a shield on the south side of the roof, prevents the blinding glare of the famous beacon from invading the Hancock at night.

The lower forty-one floors are set aside for office, parking, and other commercial use, and the forty-fifth through ninety-second floors are devoted to apartments, 705 of them ranging from studio to four-bedroom units, whose glassed-in terraces permit all-weather loafing and an uninterrupted vista. Commercial and residential tenants have their ups-and-downs separately as they use different banks of the fifty high-speed elevators (1,800 feet a minute), and five escalators. Apartment-bound passengers may travel non-stop from separate entrances at the ground floor to the "sky lobby" on the forty-fourth, which houses a restaurant, a commissary, service shops, and lounges.

Among the amenities offered by this Johnny-come-lately, which is only two blocks from a civic heirloom, the old Water Tower that somehow survived the Great Fire of 1871, are a large retail store, a swimming pool, a reflecting pool at plaza level, which becomes a skating pond in season; heated indoor parking for 1,200 cars, and completely electric heating and cooling systems.

And finally there is the observation area on the ninety-third floor, from which a million or more sightseers each year can look down on four states—Illinois, Wisconsin, Michigan, and Indiana—and then dine in lofty splendor in the gourmet restaurant that occupies the ninety-fifth and ninety-sixth floors.

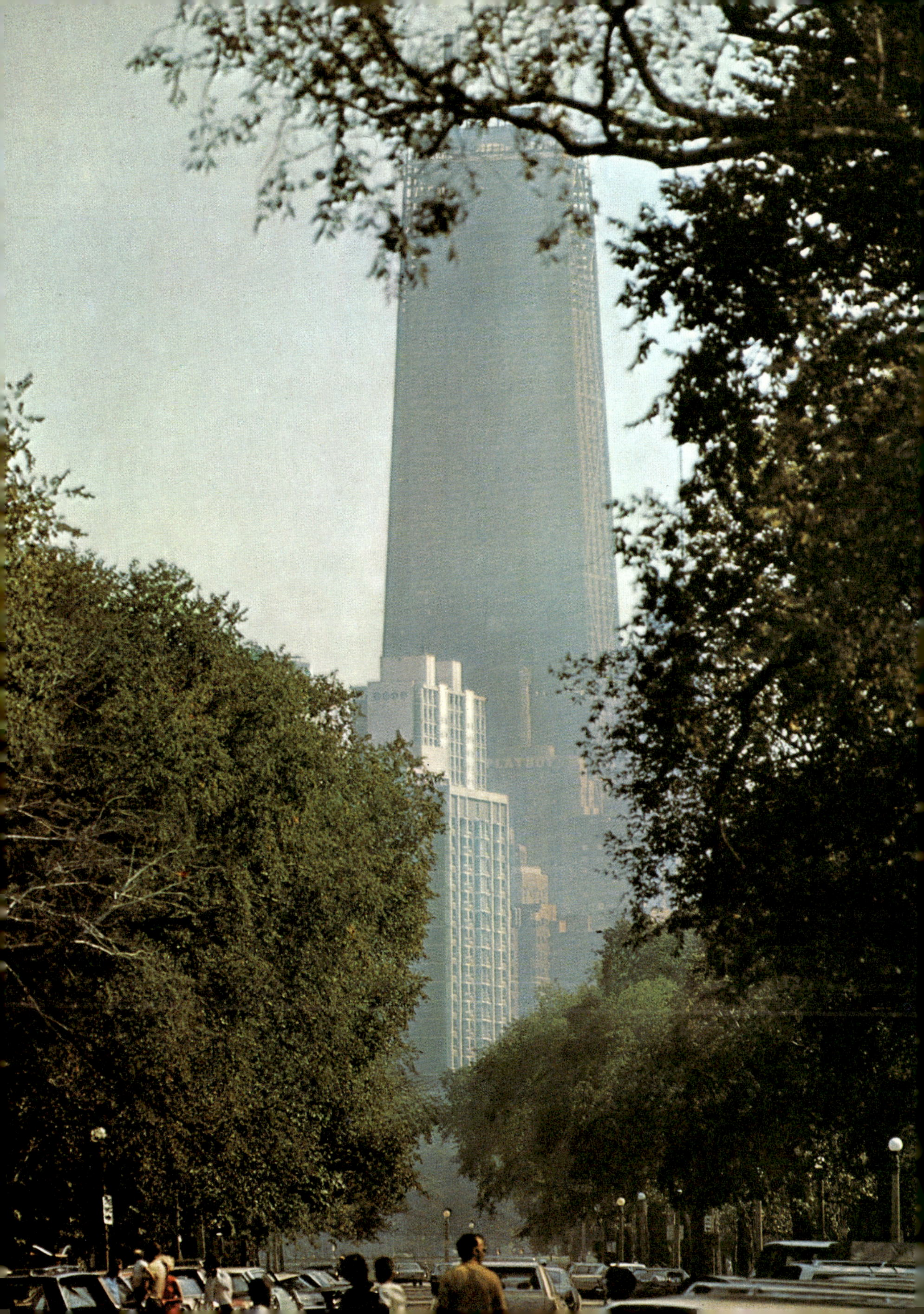

THE SKYLINE OFF LAKE MICHIGAN

It is worth taking one of the excursion trips which leave from just below the Michigan Avenue bridge, if only to gain access to such lovely aspects of the Chicago skyline as this, which is split into almost equal parts by the river. Here you may see the Equitable Building, just below the clouds in the center of the scene, and, to its right, the Wrigley Building and the Tribune Tower, which eye each other across the Magnificent Mile. Immediately to the left of the Equitable, and identifiable by the rapier-like television towers, are the twin piles of Marina City, one of Chicago's many architectural wonders. The pretty girl peering to the port side is unidentified. But she is not unusual in a town noted for such items.

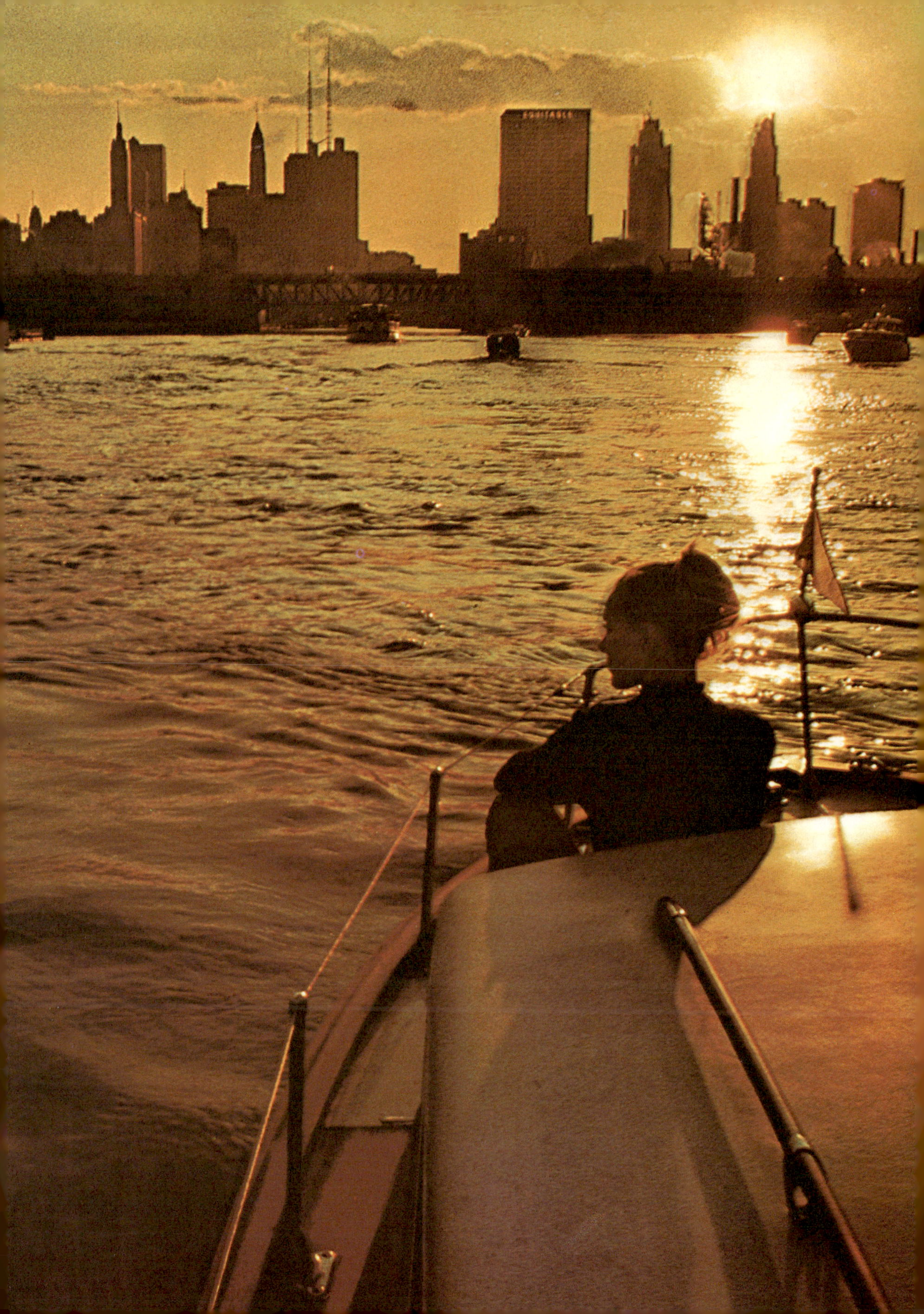

PIPER'S ALLEY, A SEGMENT OF OLD TOWN

Piper's Alley, one of the most rewarding attractions of that part of Chicago known as Old Town, began life as a bakery and would almost certainly have been torn down long since but for a happy circumstance. A few years ago someone had the imagination to visualize it as an arcade of original shops run by slightly mad business and professional folk. The entrance to Piper's Alley is off Wells Street, half a block above North Avenue, at a cobbled passageway, over which hangs a huge umbrella-light of glass. Flanking the entrance are a couple of good restaurants—The Old Farm House and That Steak Joynt—a shop dealing in folk art, and the internationally known Second City, whose alumni include Mike Nichols, Elaine May, Alan Arkin, Shelley Berman, and Barbara Harris.

Inside, at least at last reports—for Old Town's shops, eating places, and amusement spots keep changing appearance and owners—are a variety of stores where everything from candy to paper to wigs and records is sold. These include Volume I, an attractive bookshop; The Glass Unicorne, where glass gifts are blown to order; a candle shop (the Jack B. Nimble); the Bratskellar Pub, with Bratwurst and genuine antique furnishings; Le Garage, which peddles modern art at prices that will pleasantly startle you, and the Aardvark Cinematheque, which specializes in underground, experimental, foreign and classic films. One of Norman Mailer's was shown there, for example: *Beyond the Law*, in which Mailer played a police lieutenant.

It is only fair to add that Piper's Alley, varied as it is, is only a small part of Old Town, an area that swings and rocks, and is jam-packed with merry and sometimes rowdy crowds every weekend and almost any fine night. No visit to Chicago can be considered complete if you don't take in our version of Greenwich Village. At least two other bookstores on Wells must be mentioned: Barbara's, a block or so south of North Avenue, and one run by Richard Barnes, Harvard graduate and dealer in Americana, a few doors north of Piper's Alley, just beyond the parking garage. Barnes is one of the nation's outstanding rare book sellers.

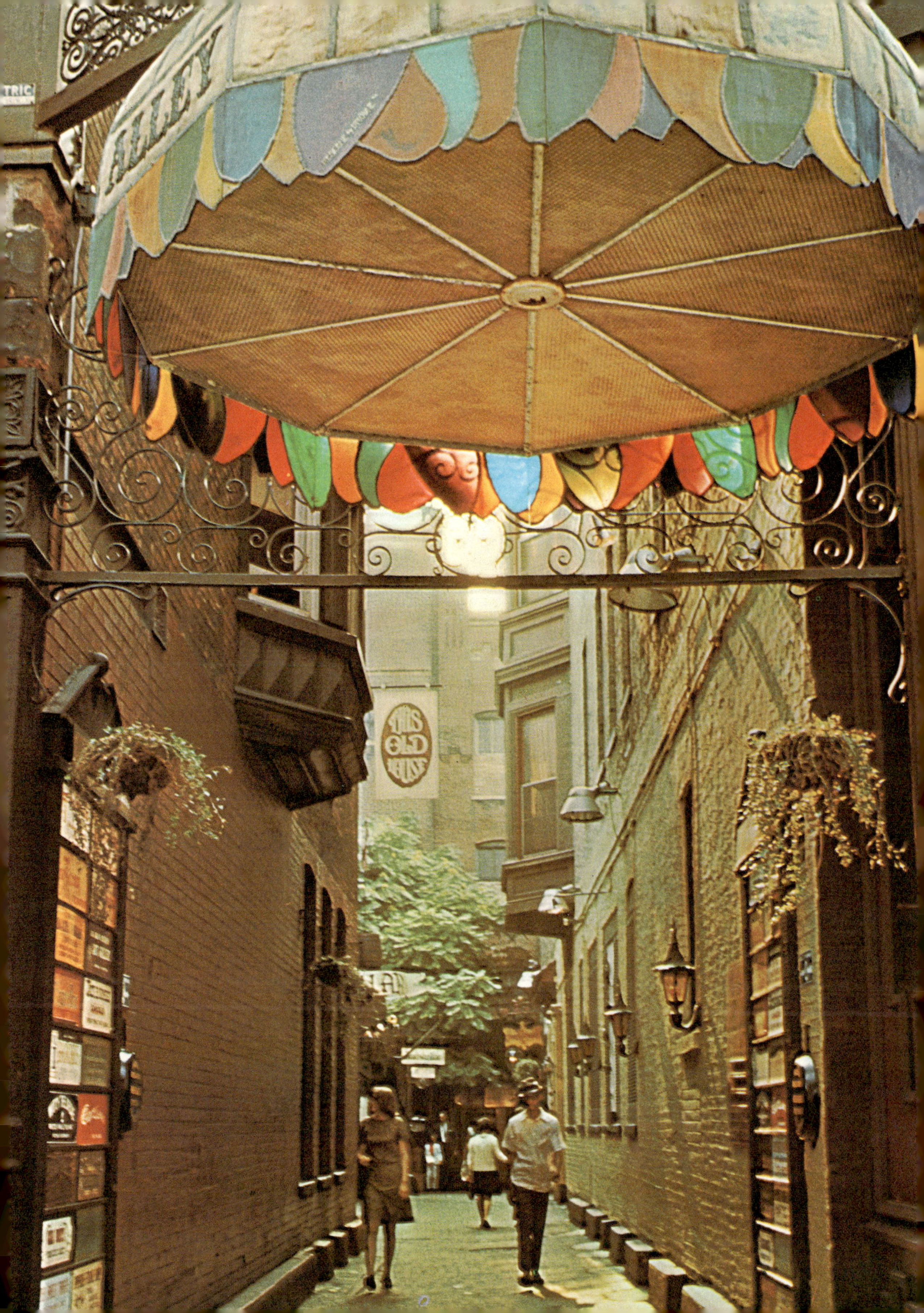
ALLEY
THIS OLD HOUSE

THE WATER TOWER, RELIC OF THE CHICAGO FIRE

When the Great Chicago Fire of October 8 and 9, 1871, devoured most of the city, destroying some 17,500 buildings and leaving more than 100,000 persons homeless, the Water Tower at Chicago Avenue and Pine Street (now Michigan) was virtually undamaged. But it was also useless, since about 3 a.m. Sunday a flaming piece of timber had landed on the roof of the supposedly fireproof pumping station, just across the street from the tower, and within an hour the roof had fallen in and the pumps were silent. This catastrophe insured the complete destruction of the North Side, because the pumping station and tower supplied all mains in the city.

    The Water Tower and rebuilt pumping station, whose cream-colored stone and crenellated battlements and turrets are a curious contrast to the neighboring Water Tower Inn, the Cinema Theater, various hotels, and the gigantic Hancock Building two blocks distant, occasion delighted comments from out-of-towners, but are largely ignored by Chicagoans, who walk by without so much as a second glance. But they are, nonetheless, a comforting link with those who lived a century ago, when the pace was slower, people were more gracious, and no one had even dreamed of splitting that blasted atom.

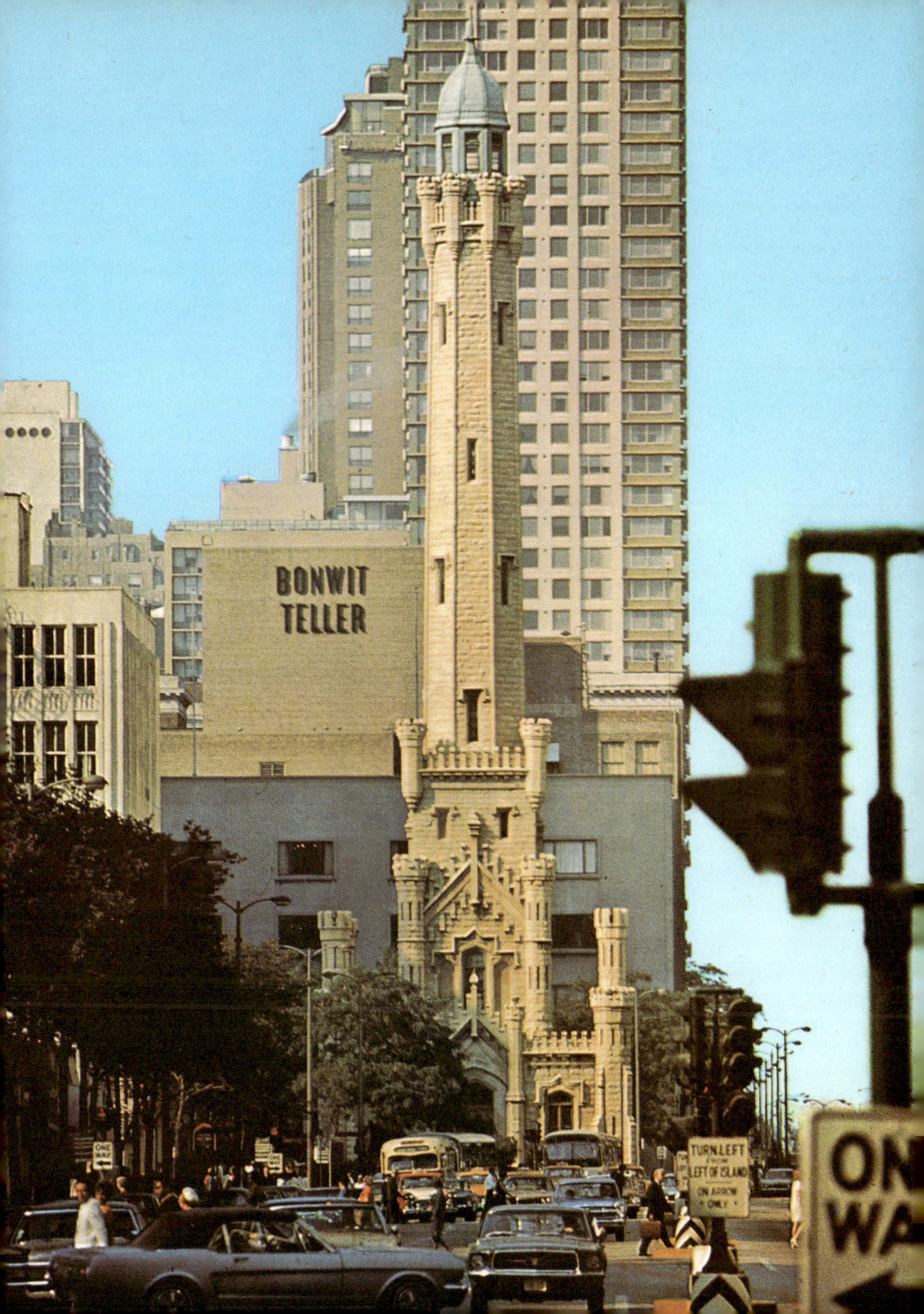
BONWIT
TELLER
TURN LEFT
LEFT OF ISLAND
ON ARROW
ONLY

THE TWINS OF MARINA CITY

Marina City advertises itself as "a city-within-a-city," and not without justification. More than 1,300 persons live in the twin towers—sixty-five stories each and 588 feet high—and they can dine, buy food, clothing, drugs or gifts; bank, bowl, ice-skate, swim, or arrange for a trip abroad without even leaving the complex.

The 3.1 acres of land, which includes 300 feet of river frontage, was bought in December, 1959, for about three million dollars. Construction was started in November, 1960, and tenants began moving into the East tower on October 14, 1962, and the West tower three months later. Credit for the unique design, said to be the first circular apartment dwellings ever built, goes to Bertrand Goldberg, a Chicago architect. Tenants park their cars in the building, which also has mooring and storage space for five hundred motorboats.

The television antenna on the towers belong to Channel 7 and Channel 32, and an arrangement of lights informs anyone watching of rising or falling temperatures, an approaching storm, or even how the home team came out that day—white lights a victory, green a loss, and alternate white and green a tie.

Chicagoans have called Marina City everything from two corncobs standing on end to "the gun turret", but don't let this fool you; they're proud of it. Tours of model apartments may be arranged, and there is an observation deck, open during decent weather.

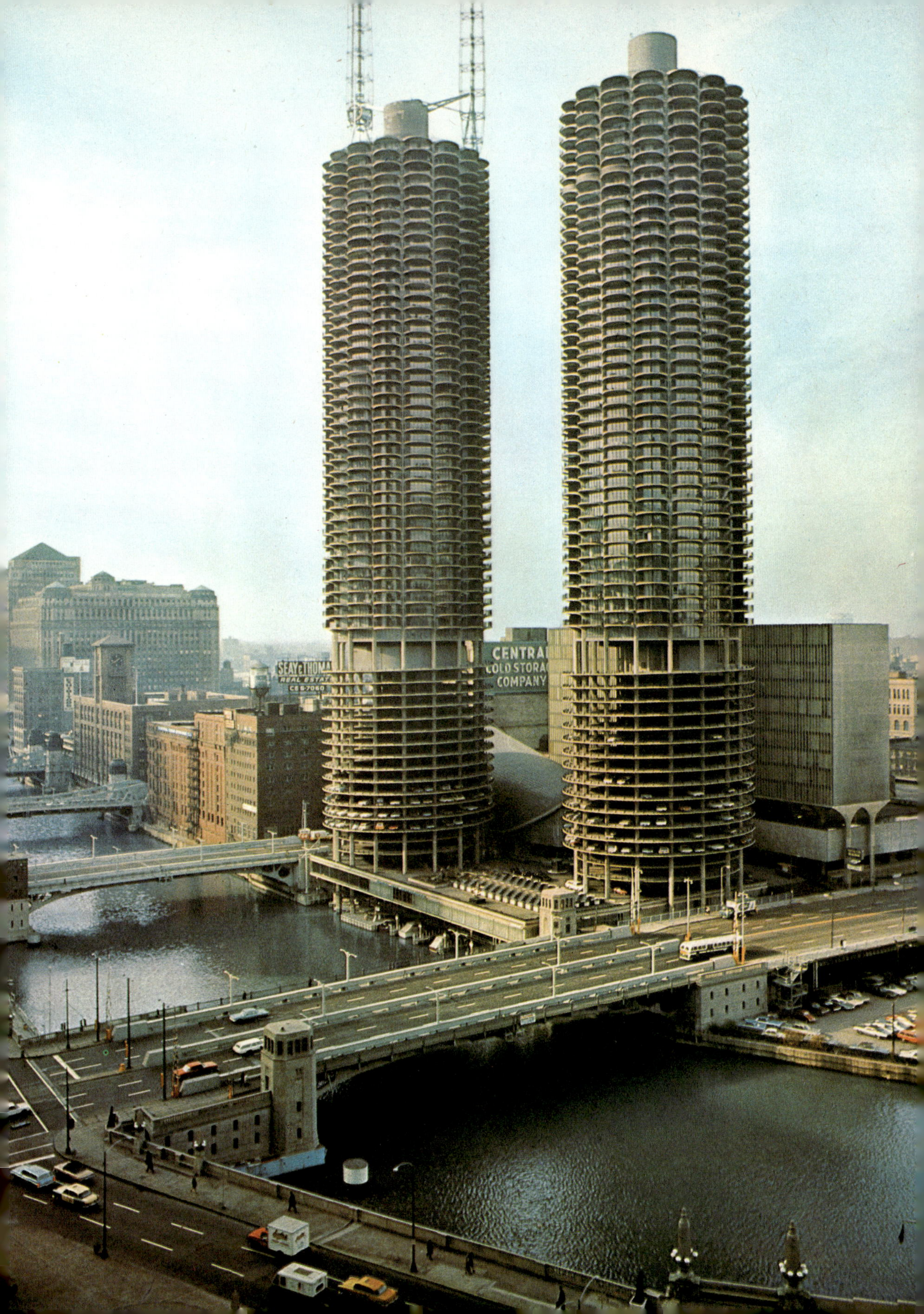
SEAY & THOMA
REAL ESTAT
CE 6-7060
CENTRA
COLD STORAG
COMPANY

THE BIG CLOCKS AT MARSHALL FIELD'S

Marshall Field and Company is one of the most famous department stores here or abroad, and the identical Field clocks you see in this photograph have a separate fame of their own. For decades Chicagoans have arranged to meet "under the clock," either at Randolph and State, which would be beneath the clock in the foreground, or at Randolph and Washington, the one a block away. The clocks are of cast bronze, weighing almost eight tons, with faces 46 inches in diameter. The hour hand is $20\frac{1}{2}$ inches long, and the minute hand 27 inches, and the lights inside serve a double purpose: to illuminate the face and to help keep the works from becoming moist. The clocks work by electricity, on an impulse sent from a master clock inside the store which corrects the subject clocks every hour. The master clock is adjusted twice daily by the Arlington time signal. A door in the bottom of the outdoor clocks may be opened to permit repairs. In 1950 an unusual rendezvous was kept beneath the clock at State and Washington: thirty women, formerly employed at Field's, met at noon in accordance with a promise made twenty years before. Field's also is quietly pleased with the fact that Norman Rockwell, illustrious artist for the *Saturday Evening Post*, used one of the clocks on the SEP cover of November 3, 1945.

See you Tuesday, usual time and place.

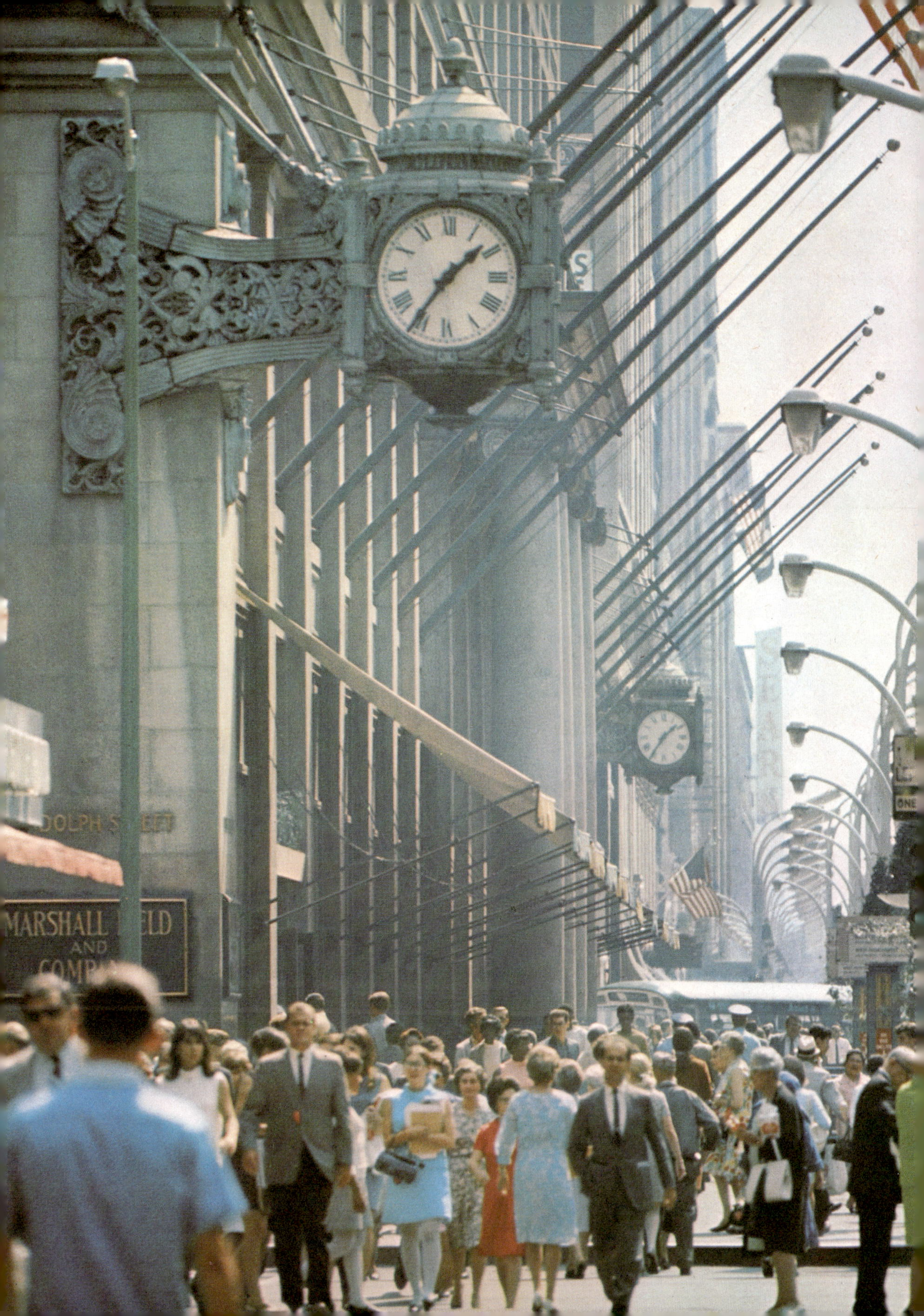
DOLPH STREET
MARSHALL FIELD
AND
COMP

THE CHICAGO FREE FAIR

A fleeting moment at the Chicago Free Fair is captured in this carefree photo. The Fair, which has been sponsored annually by the Back of the Yards Neighborhood Council for twenty-nine years, is held at 47th Street and Damen Avenue from early July through early August, and has raised thousands of dollars for this non-profit community improvement organization. The Fair offers rides, games of chance, free eye and tuberculosis examinations, inoculations against measles, tetanus, and diphtheria, and some of the strangest contests for youngsters under twelve you ever heard of: bubble-gum blowing, ice-cream eating, hot dog eating, cutest pet, most freckles, baby-crawling, turtle race (turtles may be any age), frog jumping, egg rolling, banana eating, pie eating, baton twirling, watermelon eating, twins, top spinning, fried-chicken eating, and longest pigtail. There also are attractions for adults, including various celebrity nights; your father's mustache night, Irish-American, Japanese-American, Polish-American, Scottish-American, German-American, Swedish-American, Lithuanian-American, Danish-American, Latin-American, Italian-American and Croatian-American nights; free auto giveaways, and even a money-shoveling night, whatever that is. Festivities open at 6.30 p.m. and last until 11:30 or so, and folks come pouring in from almost every part of town.

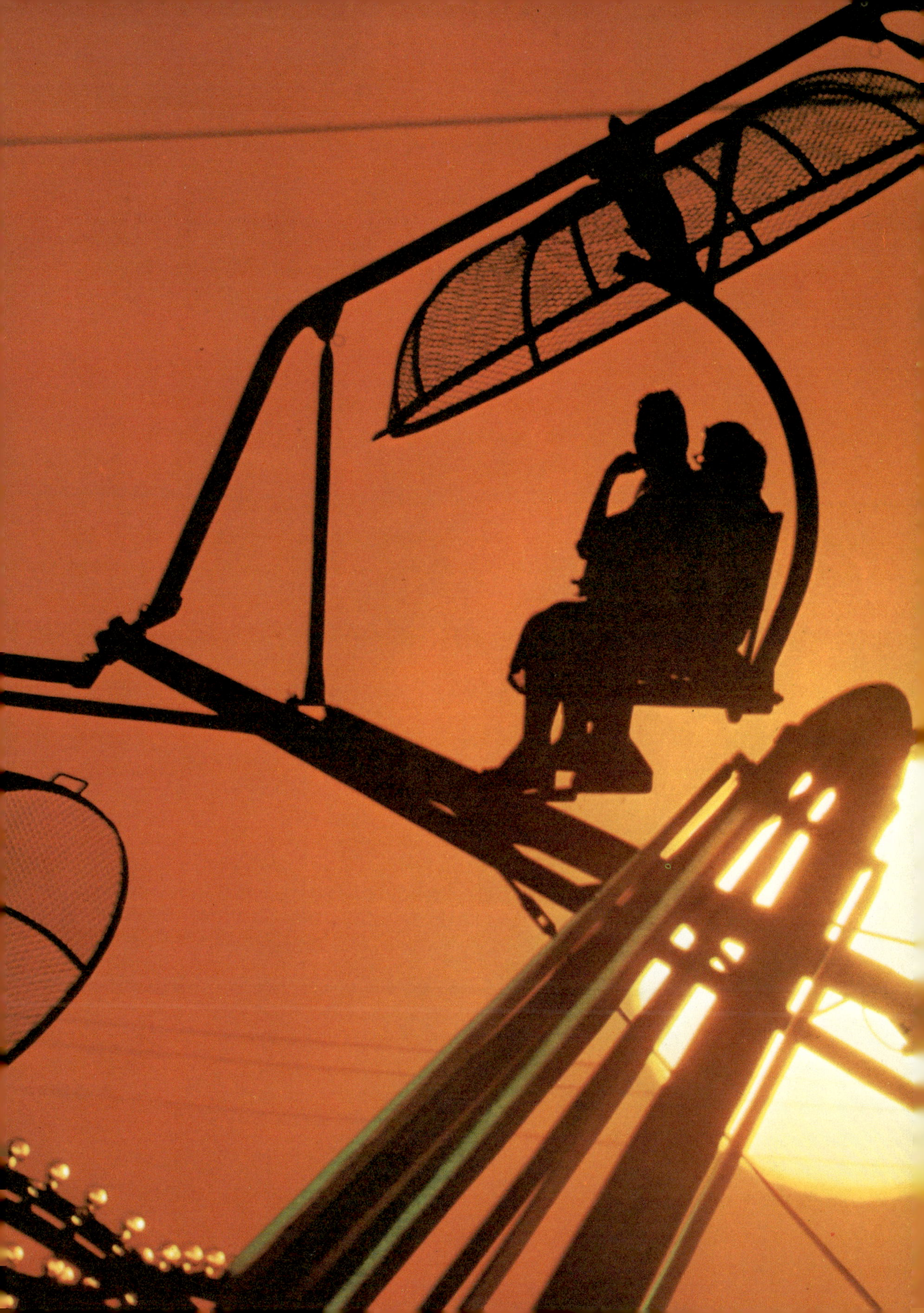

THE PICNIC THAT TIES UP THE TOWN

Thirty-nine years ago Robert S. Abbott, editor and publisher of the *Chicago Defender*, a newspaper started "in a lady's kitchen", decided to hold a picnic for the handful of small boys who were his sales crew. This first outing, held at the old duck pond in Washington Park, has grown into one of the biggest celebrations on Chicago's South Side—Bud Billiken Day. It is now open to anyone wishing to come, includes a parade with fifty or sixty floats and has attracted celebrities such as Joe Louis, Lena Horne, Mahalia Jackson, Ella Fitzgerald, Ethel Waters, the Supremes, or even two former *Defender* newsboys who made the grade—the late Nat (King) Cole and Lionel Hampton. Mrs. Marjorie Stewart Joyner, president of *Chicago Defender Charities*, says Bud Billiken is more or less based on the Chinese God of Happiness, and that Dave Kellum, city editor, and manager of the parade for many years, used to be known by that name. The parade, a "must" for many politicians, is held on the second Tuesday in August, begins near the Lake Meadows shopping area and takes about two hours to wind up in Washington Park. A basket picnic follows the march, and ice cream, cookies, pop, potato chips, hot dogs, and cake are given those who want them. There also are games and contests of all kinds. The parade is watched by huge throngs and Mrs. Joyner adds: "You can't do anything that day on the South Side but go to the parade and picnic. It ties up the whole town. It's the only time that the underprivileged, the poor, and aged adults have free entertainment during the whole year—and that's something else you can check on!"

Archie's photo shows one of the bands swinging past.

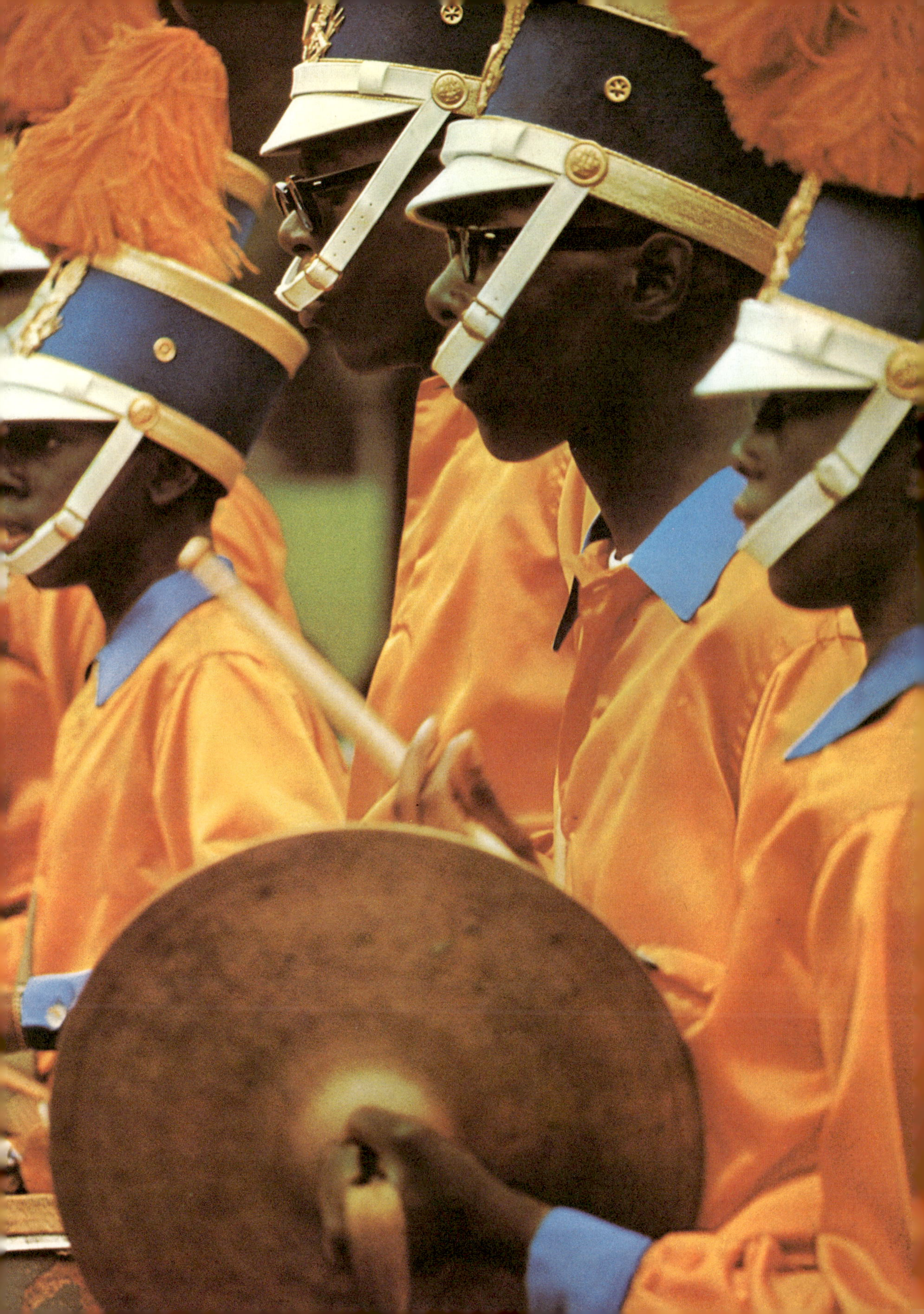

STATE STREET, THE SHOPPERS' MECCA

There are few gayer things anywhere than State Street at Christmas time. Tinsel glitters from the light standards, colored lights are abundant, Santa Claus and his helpers seem to be everywhere, and there is a spirit to the crowds of shoppers which makes them overlook the jostling, the standing in line for buses, the taxicabs that are always occupied, the fight to reach counters, and the impossibility of finding a peaceful place to eat or rest.

State Street is one of the oldest shopping centers in the world and one of the best-known. It is mentioned in the same breath with Fifth Avenue or Regent Street, Market Street or the Ginza. By night it is one of the most brightly-lighted of avenues, and by day it is impossible to find a busier corner than State and Madison. The State Street Council, which regards the nine-block, mile-long area between Wacker Drive and Congress as its particular domain, estimates that more than one hundred million customers (you are counted each time you show up) buy more than $750 million worth of goods from the stores along that stretch every year. This seems quite plausible, since the establishments include half a dozen of the finest department stores in the nation. The Council also points out that shoppers along The Street may be searching for a sable coat at $20,000 or a house-coat for a couple of bucks, and will find both.

Credit for State Street, which, as a shopping Mecca, became a century old in 1969, goes to Potter Palmer, a nineteenth century merchant prince, who bought up land along State Road in 1865, tore down the existing buildings, and built Chicago's first department store in 1869 at the corner of State and Washington—a "marble palace" that Palmer leased to Marshall Field. A few years ago land on State Street sold for as much as $21,000 a square foot, and there seems little doubt that it has increased in value since. Potter Palmer would be pleased to know how right he was.

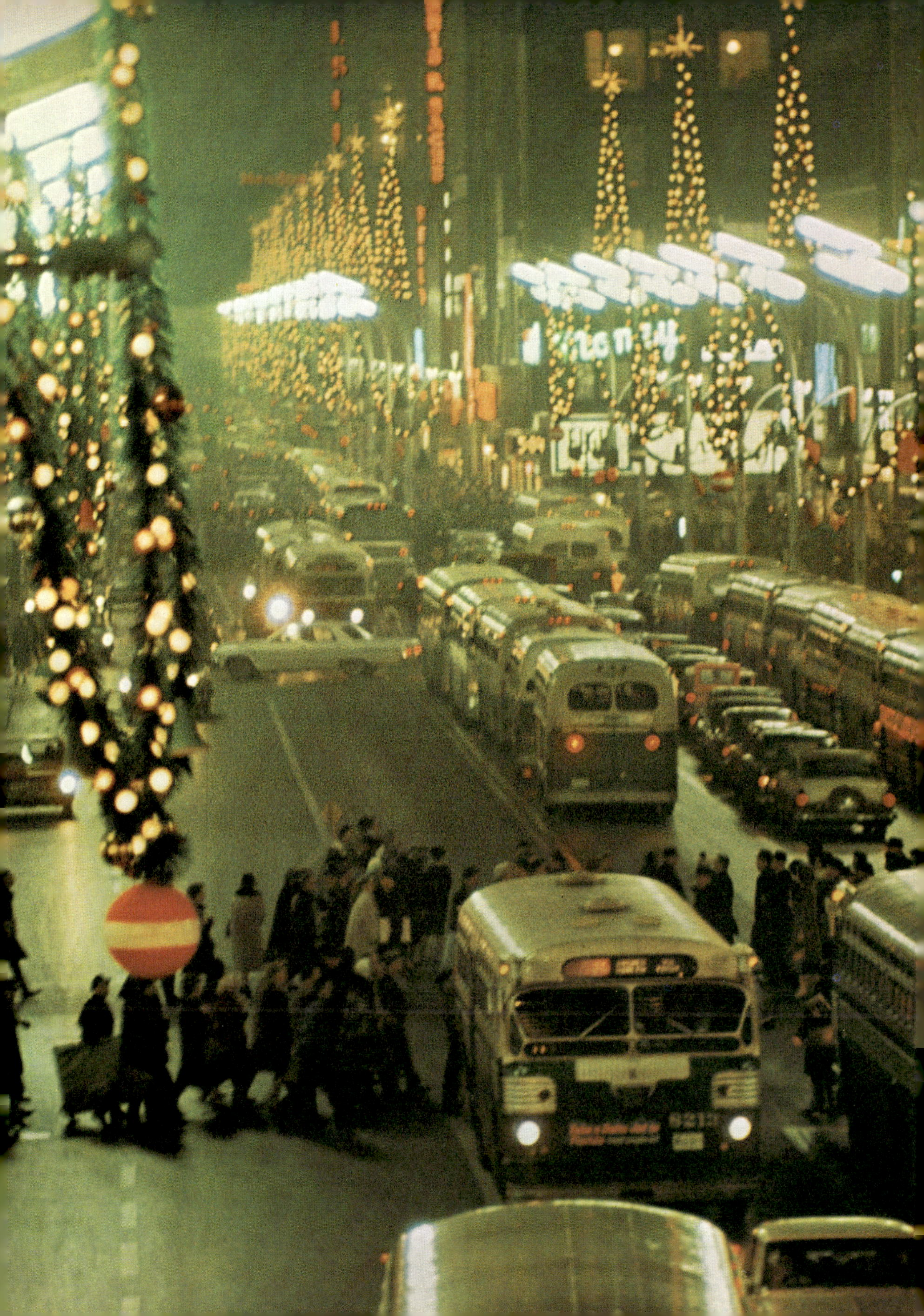

THE SHRINE OF ST. JUDE THADDEUS

St. Jude Thaddeus, according to official designation, is "the patron of hopeless cases and things despaired of." The saint's international shrine is at St. Pius V Roman Catholic Church at 1909 South Ashland Avenue, which is now in a Spanish-American parish. The church, in which these priests are saying mass, was built in 1893, on the site of an earlier St. Pius—a frame building put up in 1873 near the supposed encampment of Father Marquette during the winter of 1674–75. It is now provincial headquarters for the Dominican Order, and has six priests working among the six or seven thousand parishioners, of whom about eighty per cent are Spanish-speaking. Father Alex Kasper, OP, is in charge of the parish, and the church sponsors English classes four times weekly, taught by a teacher from the Board of Education. These attract about one hundred persons daily, five days a week, and include classes for pre-school youngsters who speak only Spanish. Father Kasper, who formerly taught philosophy at DePaul University, became interested in St. Pius after serving as a volunteer coach for the grammar school teams. He came to the parish in 1966. The church has become so well known because of the shrine of St. Jude Thaddeus that it has a mailing list of almost half a million names.

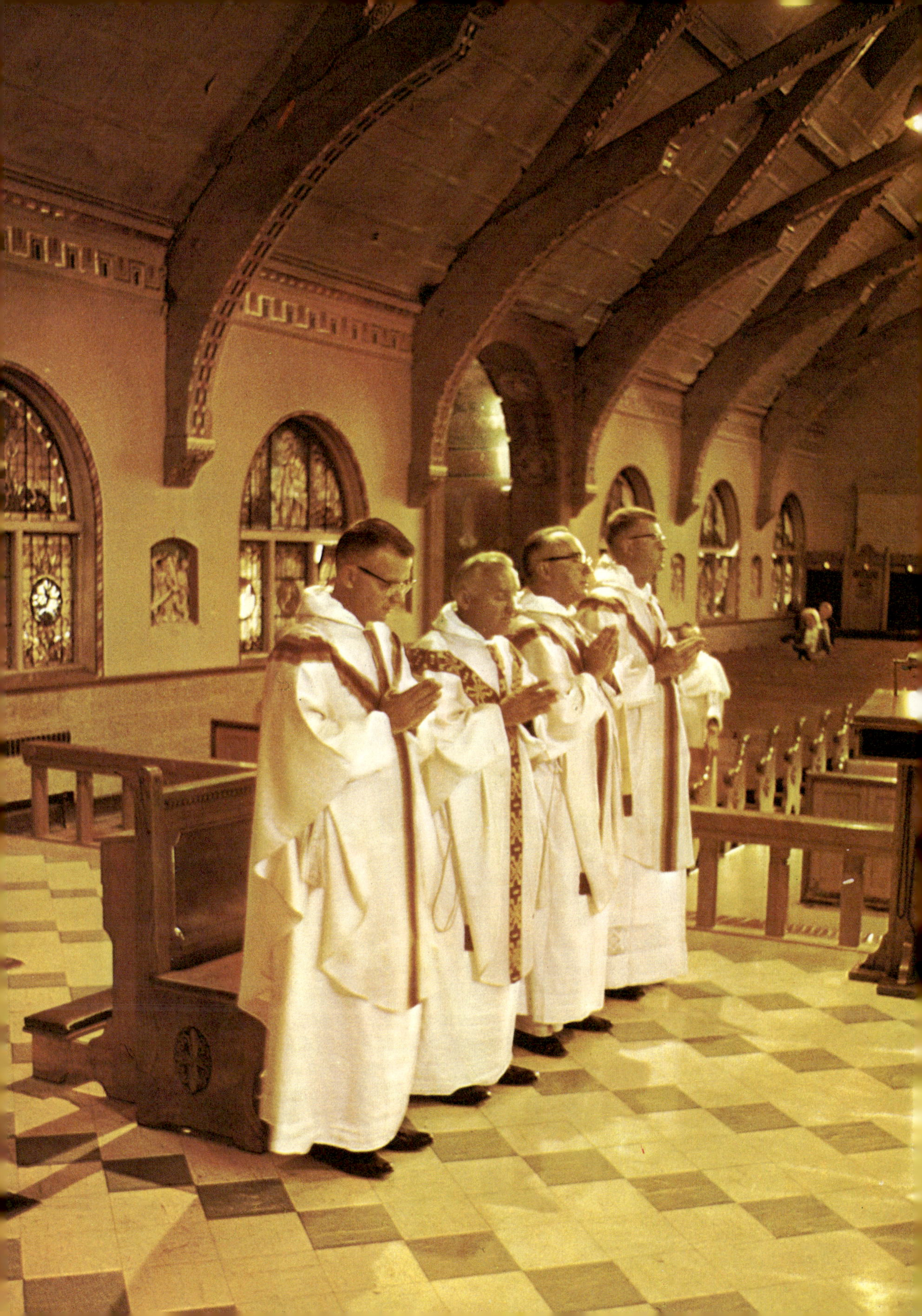

ORIENTAL CUSTOM WITH A WESTERN SLANT

Chicago's Chinatown, whose shop-windows invite your gaze in this photograph, is bounded, roughly, by Cermak Road, 24th Street, the Dan Ryan Expressway exit, and Stewart and Archer Avenues. It has a population of about 2,500 and remembers its origins on festive occasions by parades complete with fireworks, dragons, and a Chinese lion-dance. The area a few years ago was the setting for one of the town's big funerals, when final tribute was paid to Joe Moy, head of the On Leong Merchants' Association. The procession included seventy-five Cadillac limousines, eight flower cars, three brass bands (with five tubas) and two blocks of trudging mourners. Chinese-American dignitaries gathered from Detroit, New York, Baltimore, Washington, Houston, San Francisco and Minneapolis, and the cortege halted for sixty seconds in front of Lucky's Coffee Shop at Wentworth and Cermak, which Moy ran for forty years.

When Chinatown began losing population some time ago the Chinatown Redevelopment Association was formed to build new homes and attract former residents back to the neighbourhood. The scheme was eminently successful. G. H. Wang, real estate and insurance executive who was director of the redevelopment group, even managed to come up with a Chinese-sounding reason when asked why the association was formed. He said: "Better prepare for rainy weather than to patch up your corral after the cattle are gone."

Among the attractions of Chinatown are several good restaurants, stores that sell Chinese food and other Oriental wares, and the Ling Long Museum of Chinese History, now owned by Jimmy Lee, who arrived from Canton in 1937.

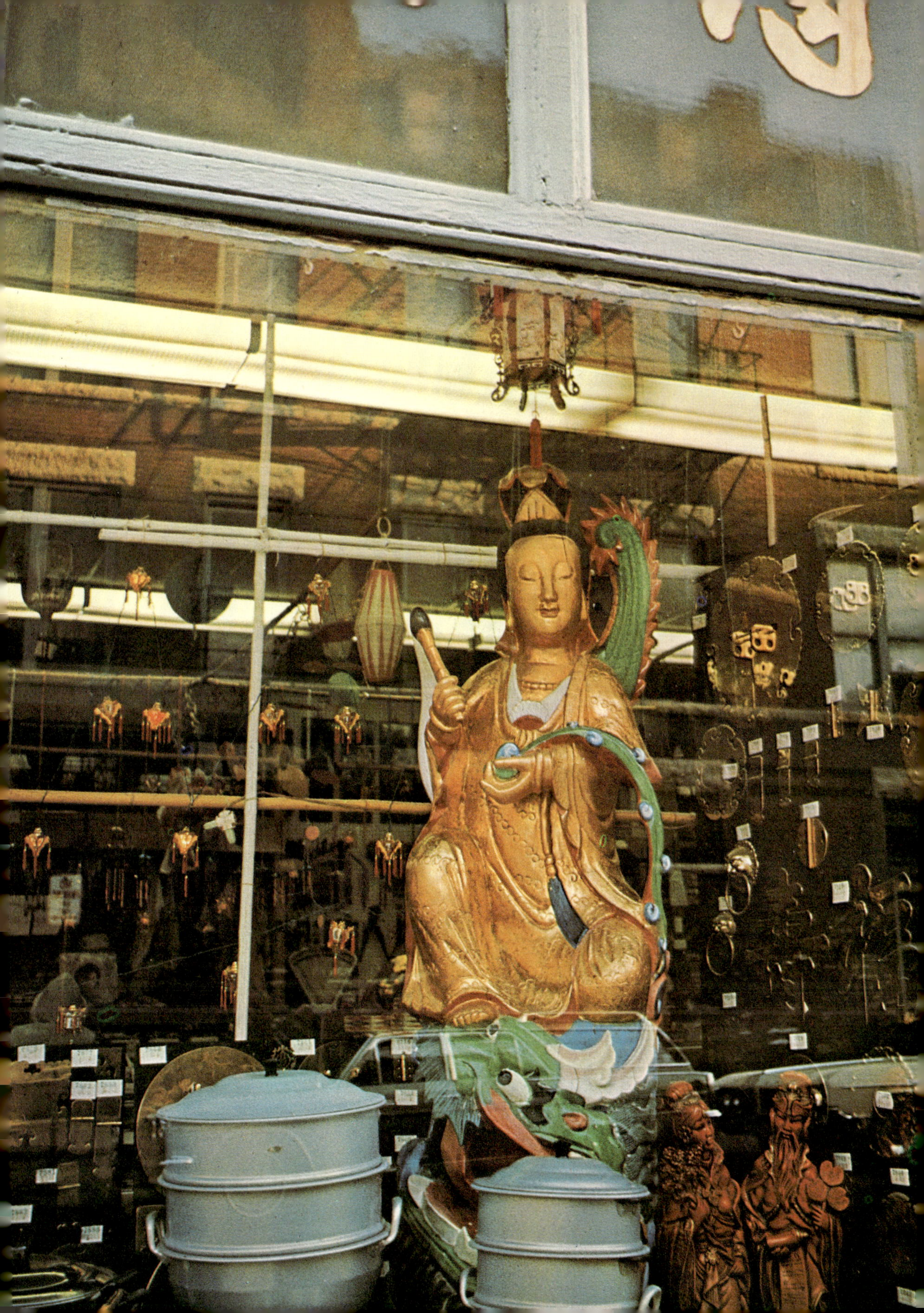

THE ART INSTITUTE AND ITS GUARDIANS

This bronze lion, one of the two that have stood guard at the Michigan Avenue entrance to the Art Institute of Chicago since 1895, was created by Edward L. Kemeys, a dentist-turned-sculptor, and purchased, with its mate, for the museum by Mrs. Henry L. Field. It weighs three tons and is a favorite and permitted perch for young visitors, which explains why the tails of both lions have become so shiny.

The Institute, one of the largest art museums in the United States, has occupied a part of its present home since two years before the lions arrived. In 1893 the Italian Renaissance building, erected at Michigan and Adams Avenues for the Congress of Religions of the World's Columbian Exposition, was turned over to the museum as its permanent quarters. This happy arrangement must be credited to Charles L. Hutchinson, president of the Institute's board of trustees, who also headed the Exposition's fine arts committee. When it was suggested that $200,000 be used for a temporary building for the Congress of Religions, which was to run from May to October, Hutchinson persuaded the museum trustees to toss another $465,000 into the pot and authorize construction of a building which would remain in use.

The original building has of course been remodeled and enlarged many times in the last seventy-five years. The Institute now offers, in addition to a priceless collection of art from all corners of the world, a professional school, a theater and dramatic school, a junior museum, and two art libraries. It is one of the most popular of the city's attractions, both for Chicagoans and for out-of-towners.

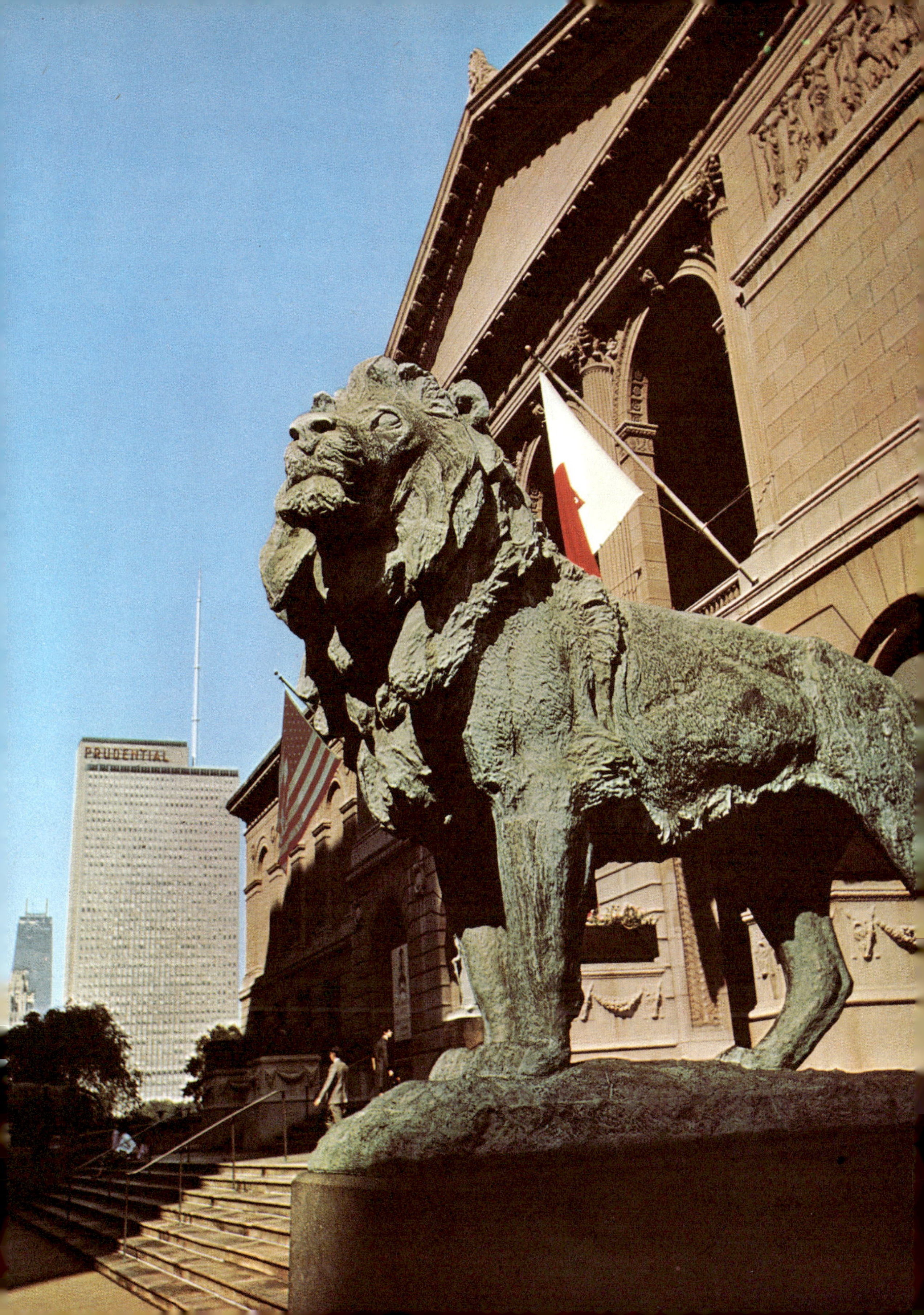
PRUDENTIAL

THE LONGEST FRESH-WATER RACE

These ghostly and graceful craft are part of a fleet that gathers each year for the Chicago-to-Mackinac race, whose 333 miles make it the longest held on fresh water. The competition, which draws entrants from all over the midwest, traditionally begins on a Saturday in July, and 1968, for example, found 197 yachts of varying sizes pitted against each other on a handicap basis. The distance has been covered in a little over twenty-eight hours, although small yachts have been known to take three times that long to reach Mackinac where scores of anxious wives gather to await their sailing husbands. All is not always fun and games. As you can see by the photograph, fog can be a factor, and in 1937 the fleet ran into winds of 60 to 80 miles an hour that kept buffeting the lake for a day and a half. That year the wives waited a long time. The race is carefully regulated in the interests of safety, however, and a coastguard cutter always is on hand to shepherd home any cripples or strays.

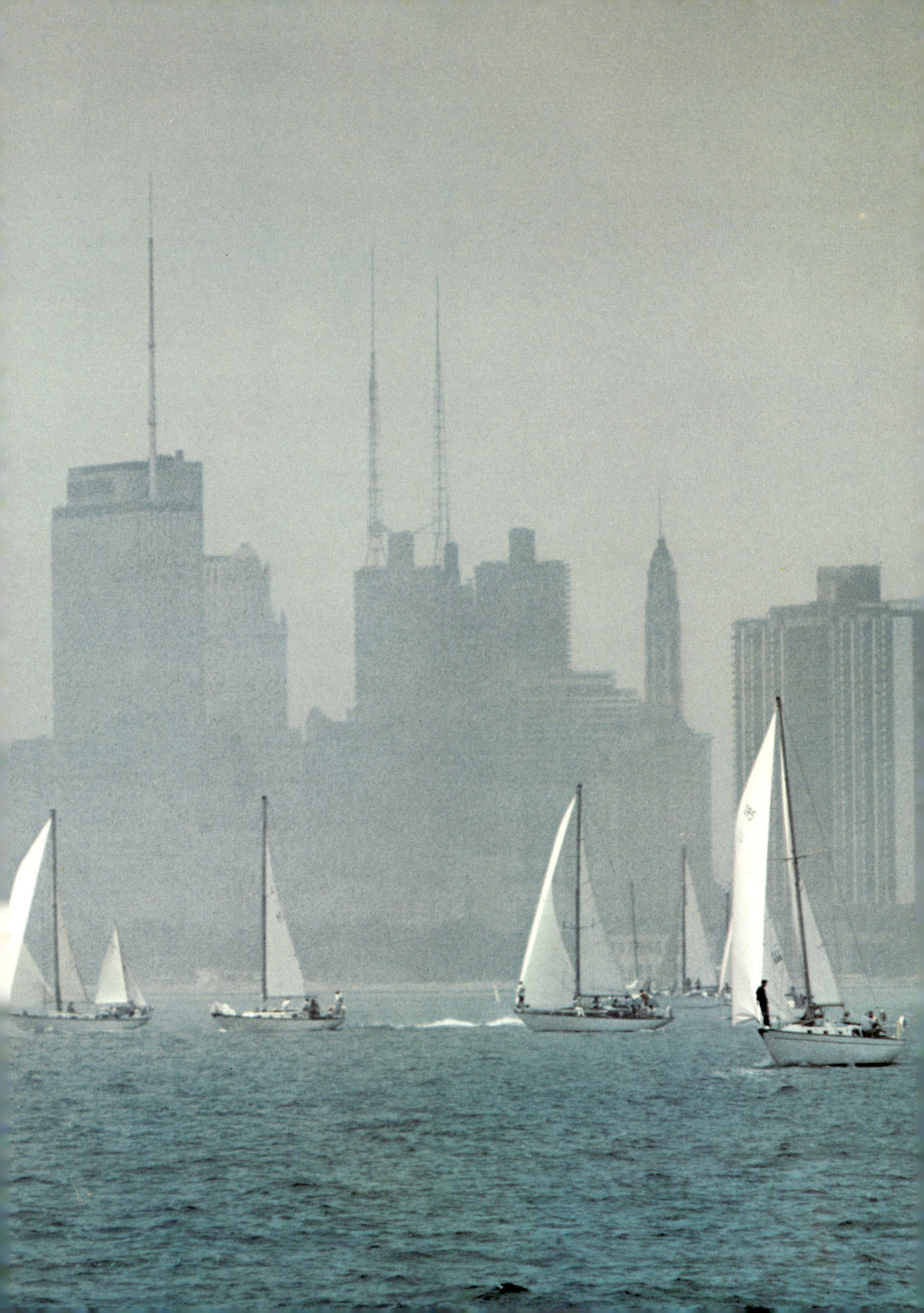

FISH OF EVERY SHAPE AND COLOR

These steps lead to the John Shedd Aquarium, the world's largest, on South Lake Shore Drive. It contains examples of virtually every aquatic animal except the mermaid and the Loch Ness monster, although either would be eagerly welcomed. It is home to between 5,000 and 7,500 specimens, including turtles, fish of every shape and color, tiny sea-horses, a penguin or so, and everything else that lives in water, can stand captivity, and is small enough to fit into one of the tanks without being cramped for space. The building is closed only on Christmas and New Year's Day, and children pay nothing at any time. Adults are admitted free only on Thursday, Saturday, and Sunday. Other days they are charged 25 cents—which still makes a visit one of the best bargains in town. The Aquarium should be part of a tour that can easily include the nearby Field Museum of Natural History and Adler Planetarium.

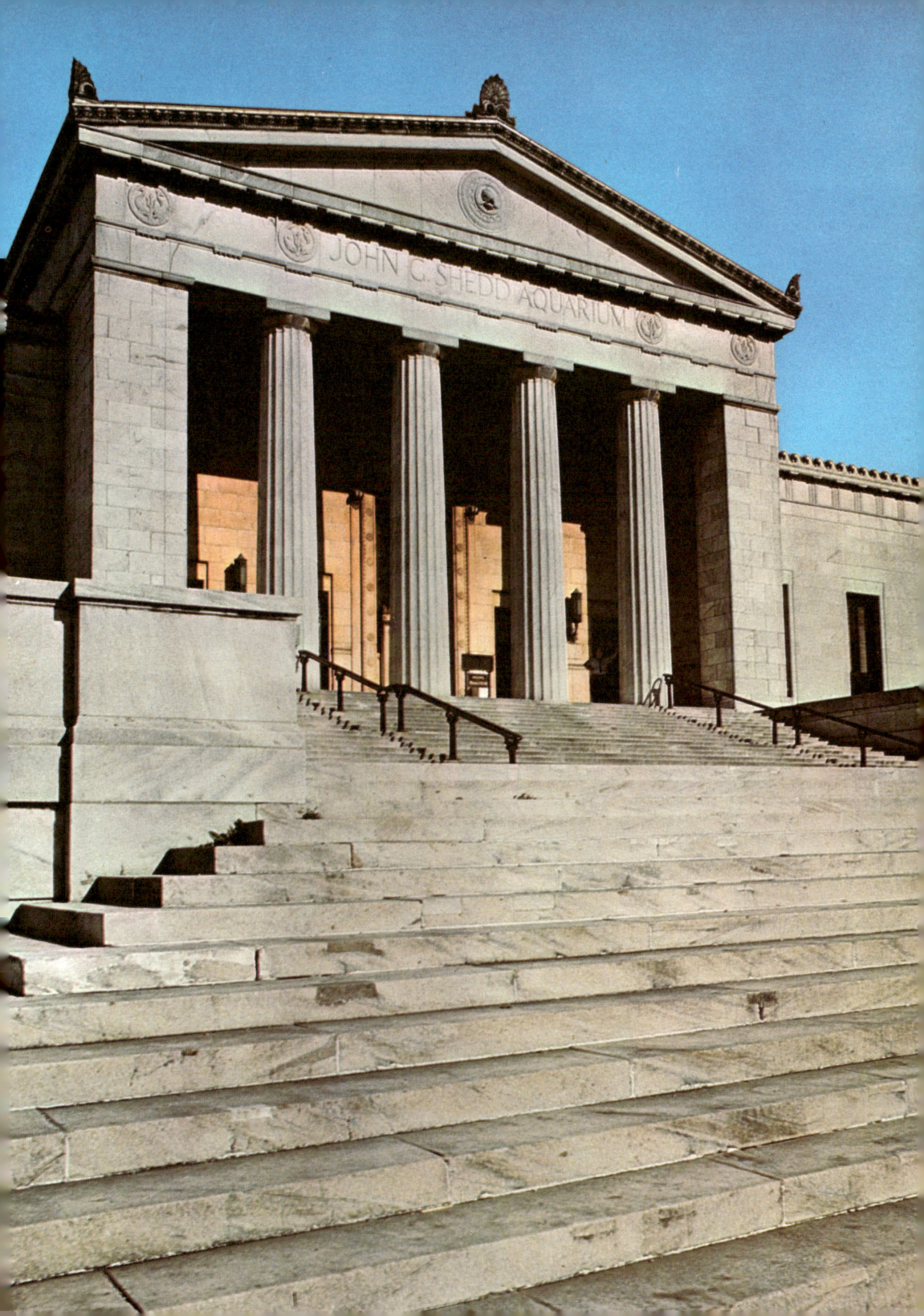
JOHN G. SHEDD AQUARIUM

TRAFFIC ON THE IKE

If this were rush hour you would be well advised to continue on home in your flying machine, because Chicago's expressway system is no more capable of handling a mass outpouring of vehicles than is that of any other city. This particular segment of highway, with its sweeping lines and momentarily modest traffic flow is part of the Eisenhower Expressway in the vicinity of the Circle Campus of the University of Illinois. The Eisenhower, incidentally, originally was named the Congress Street Expressway. But when the Northwest Expressway became the Kennedy in honor of the martyred President someone must have said, "Hey! fair's fair!", and a few weeks later the west-bound freeway was renamed the Eisenhower, or the Ike, thus preventing any further partisan outcry.

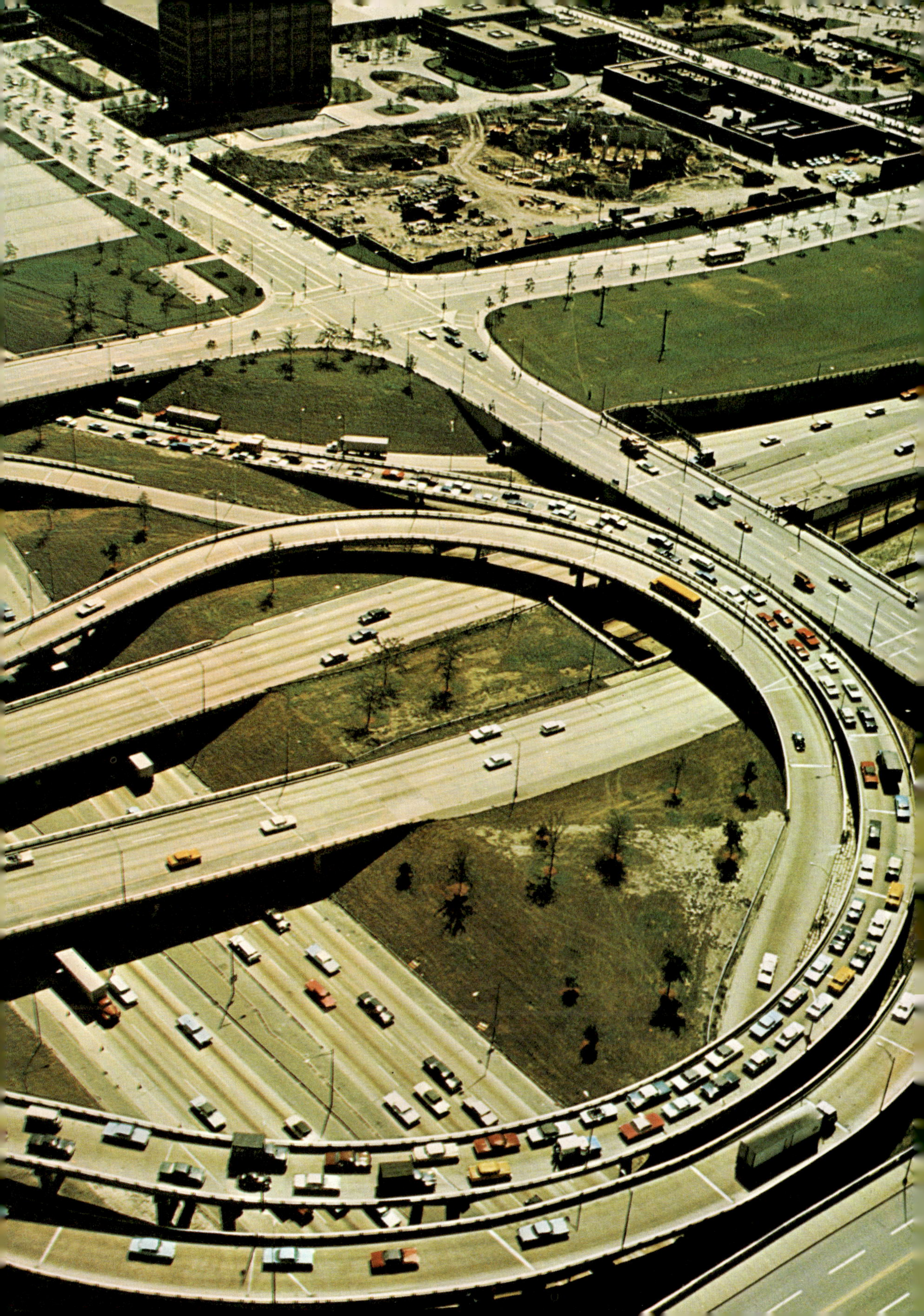

A HAVEN FOR BUDDING LAWYERS

It is possible that those attending the Northwestern University Law School will be better lawyers, or at least better-adjusted ones, because of the formal garden, permanently endowed by Mrs. Hortense Mayer Hirsch, whose mother, Mrs. Levy Mayer, paid for the construction of one of the buildings that form the quadrangle surrounding the garden.

A drive for funds to begin the law school on the Downtown Campus was lagging in the early twenties, even though William Jennings Bryan, an alumnus, spoke at the sixtieth anniversary dinner. But in the autumn of 1923 Dean John H. Wigmore received the following letter from Mrs. Rachel Mayer, widow of a prominent attorney.

"It is my earnest desire to erect, in the city of Chicago, a suitable memorial to my beloved husband; and I can think of no more appropriate and enduring form than a building, in which shall be educated the future generation of lawyers, who will learn thus to revere his memory in the great city where his career was made. I have, therefore, set aside the sum of $500,000 to erect a 'Law School' for Northwestern University, on the McKinlock Memorial Campus. That is all I have to say, except to add that, the sooner the building is erected, the better I shall be satisfied. I intend to go abroad again some time next year and I do not wish, if possible, to leave this country until I have seen the 'Levy Mayer Hall' with my own eyes."

The Elbert H. Gary Law Library, housed in another of the quadrangle buildings, is one of the six greatest law collections in the United States.

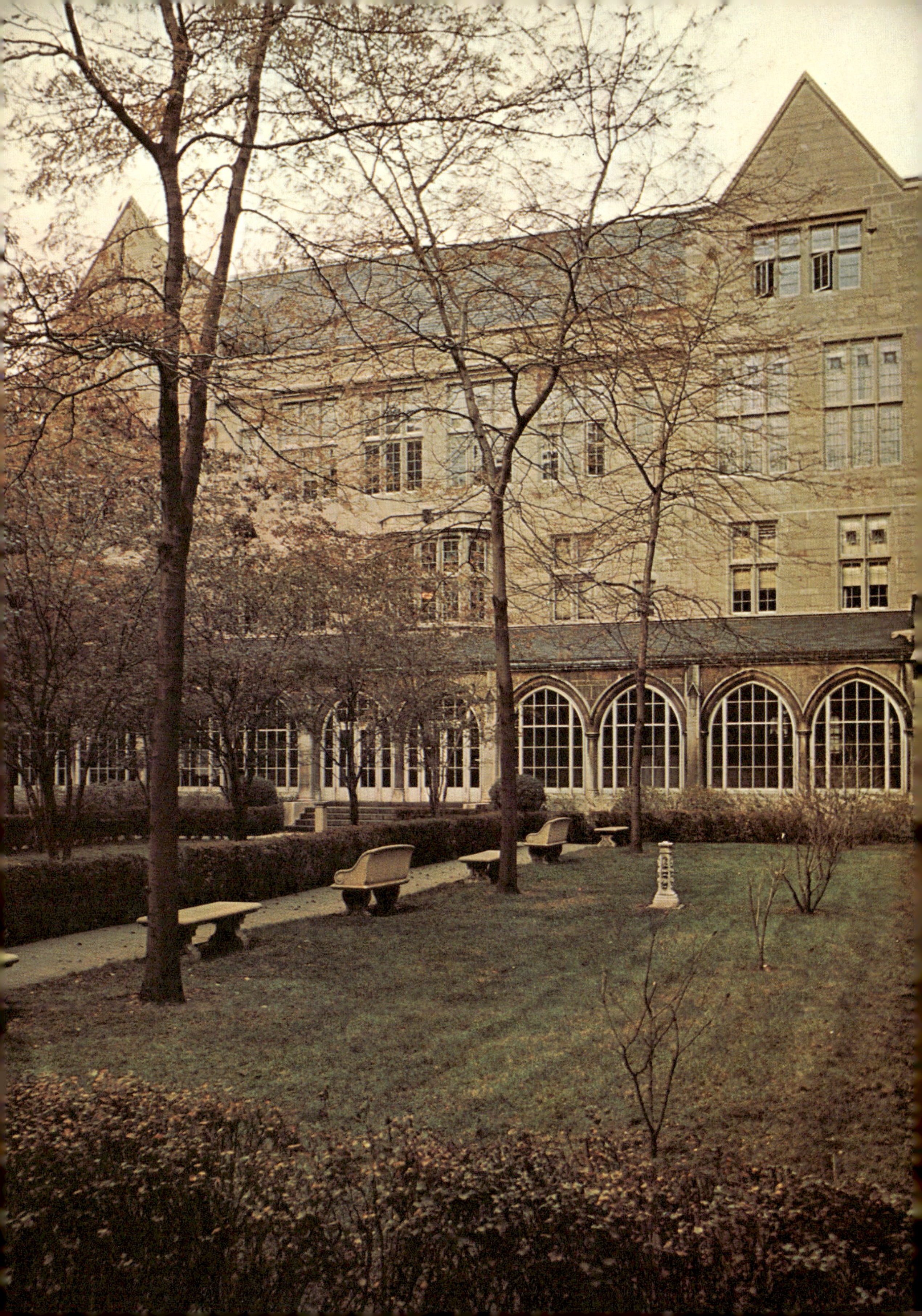

THE CAMPUS AT CHICAGO CIRCLE

It is pleasant to remember that the result of an acrimonious debate over an urban renewal project is Chicago Circle Campus of the University of Illinois, which opened in 1965 and is bounded by Roosevelt Road (12th Street), Morgan Street, and the Eisenhower and Dan Ryan Expressways.

This is a "commuter" school, as the *Student Handbook* makes completely clear: "The University of Illinois at Chicago Circle was developed to serve the needs of students who can travel to and from the campus on a daily basis. It is assumed that most students will be living at home with their families, or, if minors, in accommodations of which their parents would approve."

The University is made up of five colleges: architecture and art, business administration, education, engineering, and liberal arts, and a school of physical education. The campus buildings are clustered around the lecture center, with its roof-top amphitheater which has 2,500 open-air seats. Circle Campus, whose attractions include historic Hull House, founded in Victorian times by Jane Addams as a social service center, will repay a visit. If you like, there are conducted tours at frequent intervals.

Jory Graham, in her book *Chicago, An Extraordinary Guide*, sets down a curious and vaguely disturbing fact:

"The traffic jam on the walks at the ten-minute breaks between classes was created by the architects, deliberately, in the hope of offsetting the sense of isolation students at commuter campuses usually feel. If at no other time, students and faculty are at least physically close during the hourly shift from classrooms in one building to another."

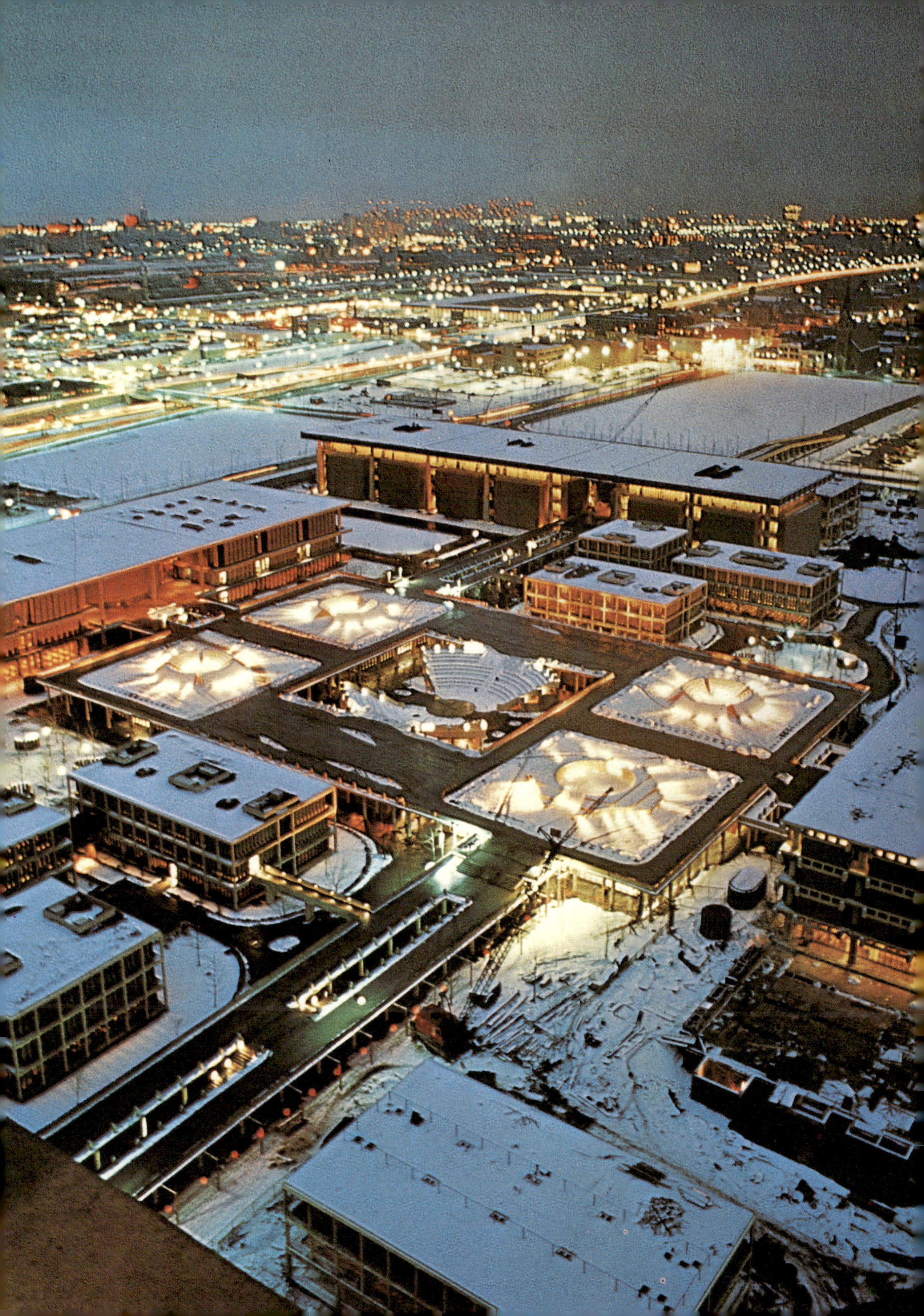

A PROMENADE UP THE AVENUE

Michigan Avenue, looking north from Randolph Street, at whose southwest corner you will find the rambling Chicago Public Library, offers one of the most enticing of all Chicago vistas. In this photograph you can see the river bridge, which bears a plaque telling about Fort Dearborn, whose outlines may be found in brass on the sidewalk and roadway near by; the Wrigley Building, just across the river to the left, and the soaring Gothic tower that is the *Chicago Tribune* building, almost opposite on the right.

Michigan Avenue, most of whose fine shops are to be found in that stretch known as the "magnificent mile," is a favorite for window-shoppers, hand-in-hand strollers, and out-of-towners with cameras. Pressroom employees from the *Chicago Tribune* in their paper hats sit leaning against the stone balustrades and watch the girls go by. That's in *fine* weather. On wintry, blustering days, Michigan Avenue is a test of endurance.

The 333 Building is headquarters for one of Chicago's most exclusive clubs, The Tavern, and also for one of the nation's outstanding book, map, and print dealers, Kenneth Nebenzahl, with whom you can spend $20 or $50,000 for a single item of Americana. From this spot the walk northward offers a variety of attractions.

It will take you past bridge, Wrigley, Prudential, and *Tribune*, as well as the Sheraton–Chicago Hotel, with its spectacular Camelot dining room; Diana Court, which boasts the superb Diana Fountain by Carl Milles; a Kroch's and Brentano's branch bookstore, Stuart Brent's new bookstore, modeled on Blackwell's in Oxford; Saks Fifth Avenue, Woolworth's, the old Water Tower, the Cinema Theater (a quarter-block right at Chicago Avenue), the Fourth Presbyterian Church, one of the loveliest in town; the John Hancock Building, Continental Plaza Hotel, the Playboy (formerly Palmolive) building, with its great Playboy (formerly Lindbergh and then Palmolive) beacon; the Drake Hotel, Jacques' French restaurant, and other enticing places. Not, in short, a promenade to be missed.

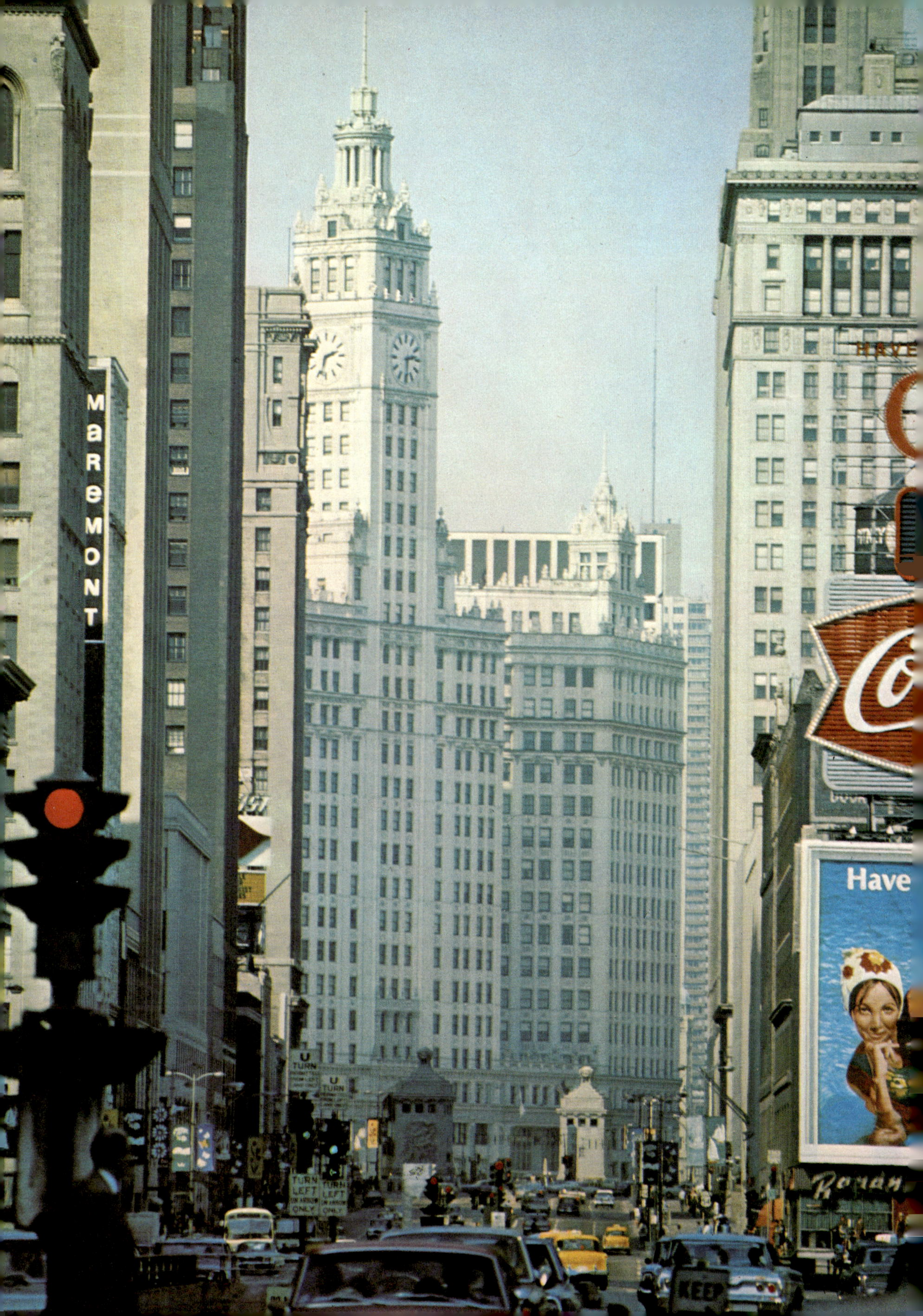
MAREMONT
Have

WHERE THE NAVAL RECRUITS COME FROM

These are young Americans from all over the country, shown during one of the every-Friday (May to October) graduation exercises at the Great Lakes Naval Training Center near Waukegan, in the far northern suburbs. The ceremonies, which include such spectacles as precision marching and the color-guard, are favorites with sightseers and of course members of the young sailors' families. Tours of the Ninth Naval District facilities at Great Lakes may be arranged for groups. Cruises to all parts of the world are arranged for the trainees you see here.

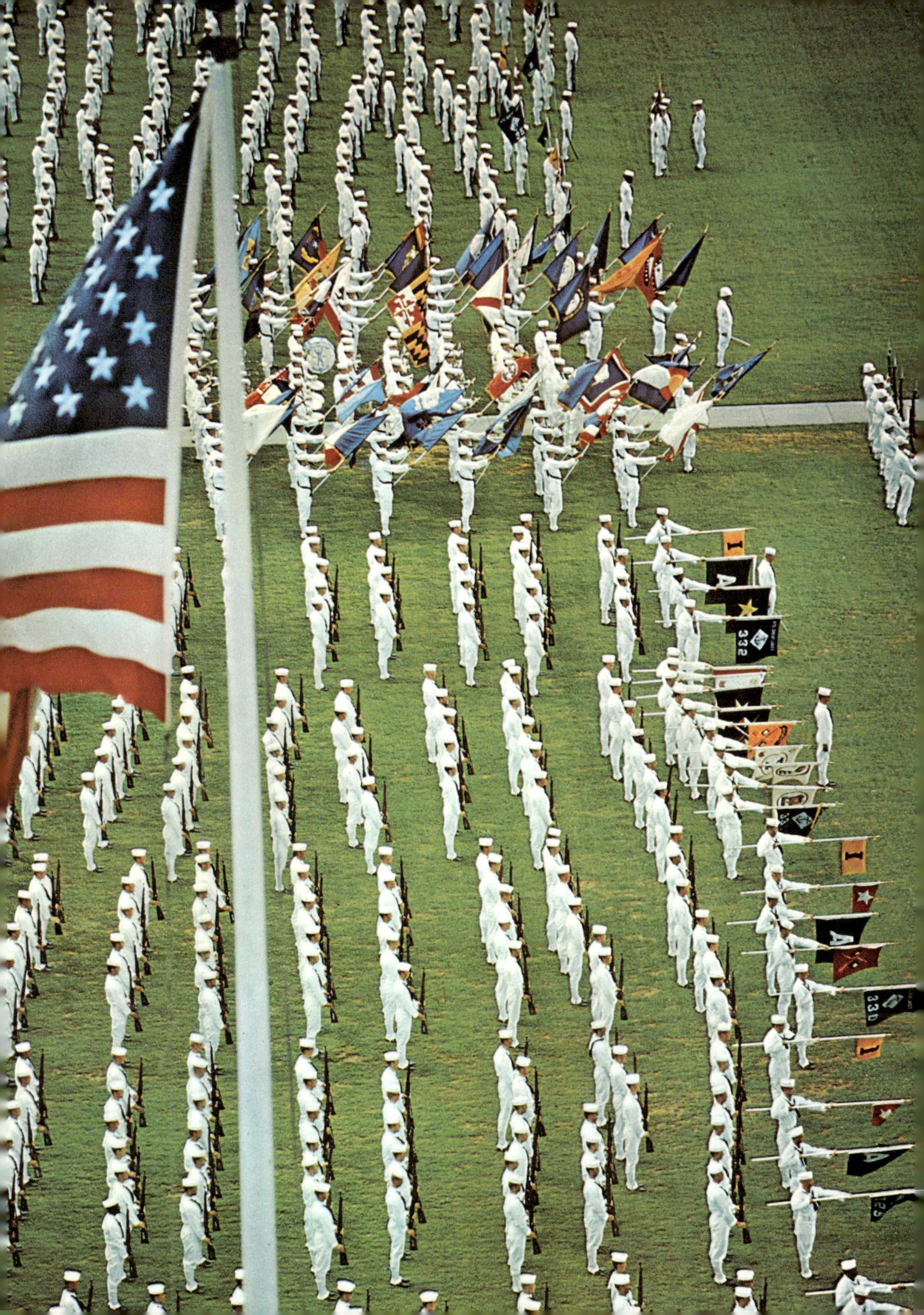

ROCKEFELLER CHAPEL AND ITS BELLS

The University of Chicago Chapel was dedicated October 28, 1928, and its name changed to the Rockefeller Memorial Chapel in 1937, after the death of John D. Rockefeller. On the day of dedication John D. Rockefeller, Jr., announced a gift of one million dollars for the Chapel's endowment, the money to be used "to promote religious idealism through the broadest and most liberal development of the spiritual forces centering in and radiating from this Chapel." On Thanksgiving Day, 1932, a carillon of seventy-two bells was dedicated in memory of Mrs. Laura Spelman Rockefeller, bringing to $2,282,000 the total cost of Chapel and carillon.

If you want further details on the Chapel, a seven-page, single-spaced, mimeographed sheet has been prepared by the University's public relations people, which gives measurements (265 feet long, 120 feet wide at the transept, and 102 feet high); material used (solid masonry faced with Indiana blue limestone); weight (32,000 tons for walls, tower and roof) and height of tower (207 feet), as well as other incidental data, including the fact that the interior woodcarving was done by Alois Lang of Oberammergau, Germany, and is not solely biblical or religious in theme.

But the carvings, windows, sculptures, coats of arms, banners and other decorations are far too numerous and complex to demand explanation. Let's conclude with the University's own estimate of the Chapel as "the most enduringly impressive structure on campus" and this final anonymous paragraph:

"Without ostentation, but with soaring emphasis, the Chapel presents a continuing inspiration to the students, faculty, and strangers within her gates, seeming to say, indeed, 'What is past is prologue.'"

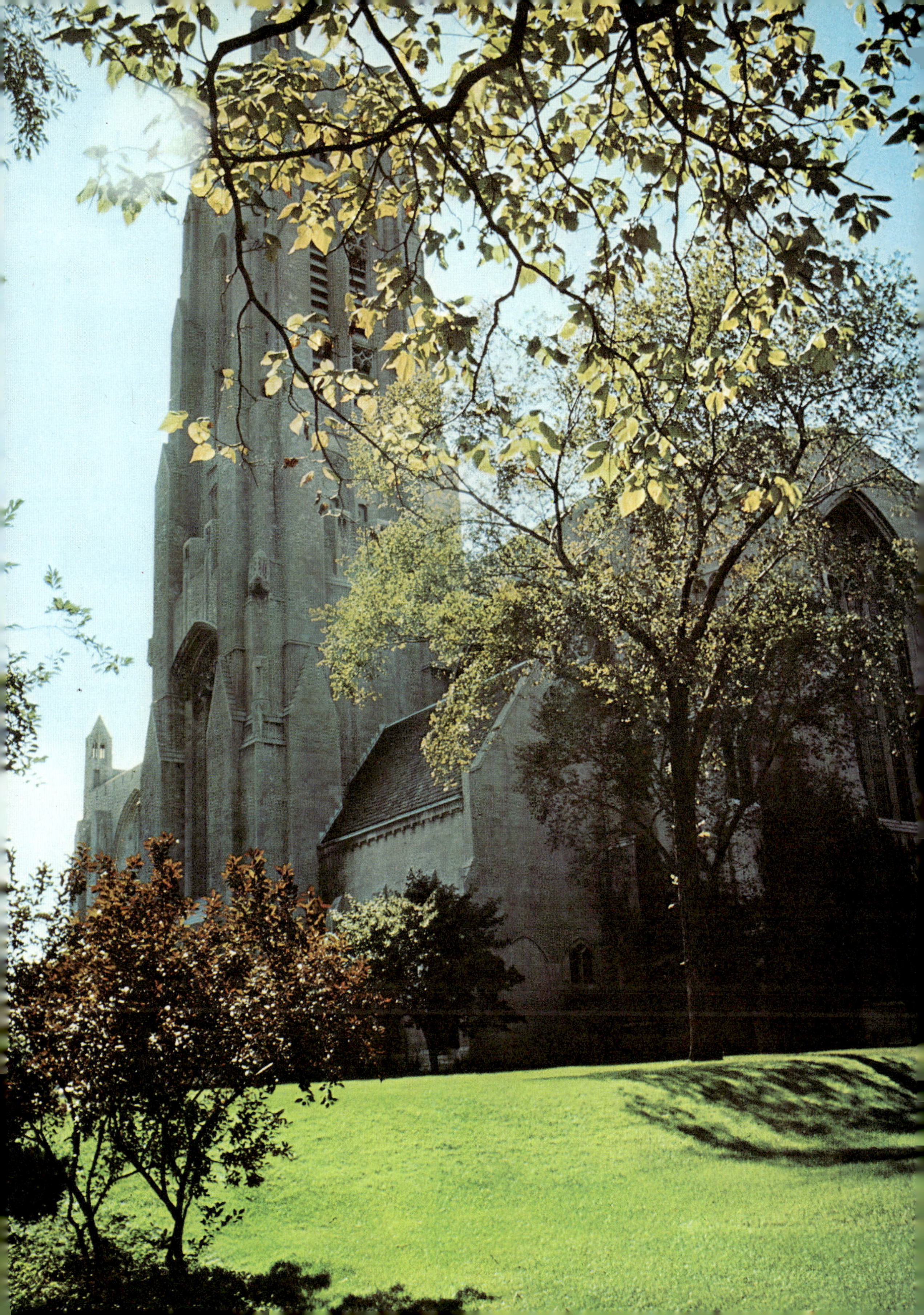

PLANTS FOR BEAUTY AND FOR USE

You are in the Palm House of the Garfield Park Conservatory, one of the city's most impressive showplaces, located at Central Park Avenue and Lake Street. It is one of the finest public-owned botanical gardens in the world, and its five thousand species of plants and flowers are valued at more than one and a half million dollars.

The Palm House, largest of the several buildings on the $4\frac{1}{2}$-acre conservatory grounds, is 250 feet long and contains 125 kinds of palms, including half a dozen Royal Palms which stand beside the reflecting pool.

Other attractions at Garfield Park Conservatory are The Fernery, which the late Lorado Taft once called "the most beautiful room in America," the Horticultural Hall, where four major shows are held each year; the Aroid House, whose temperature never dips below 70 degrees, and which contains a small pool fashioned to represent an extinct volcano, and the Cactus House, where four hundred species of desert plants are on view, among them the Saguaro or Giant Cactus, which reaches a height of almost 60 feet.

Students find the Economic House of particular interest, since all plants growing there have commercial value. These include citrus trees, the chicle plant, fig, olive, sugar cane, cinnamon, and avocado and numerous sweet-smelling flowering plants whose blooms are used in the manufacture of perfumes.

Admission is always free.

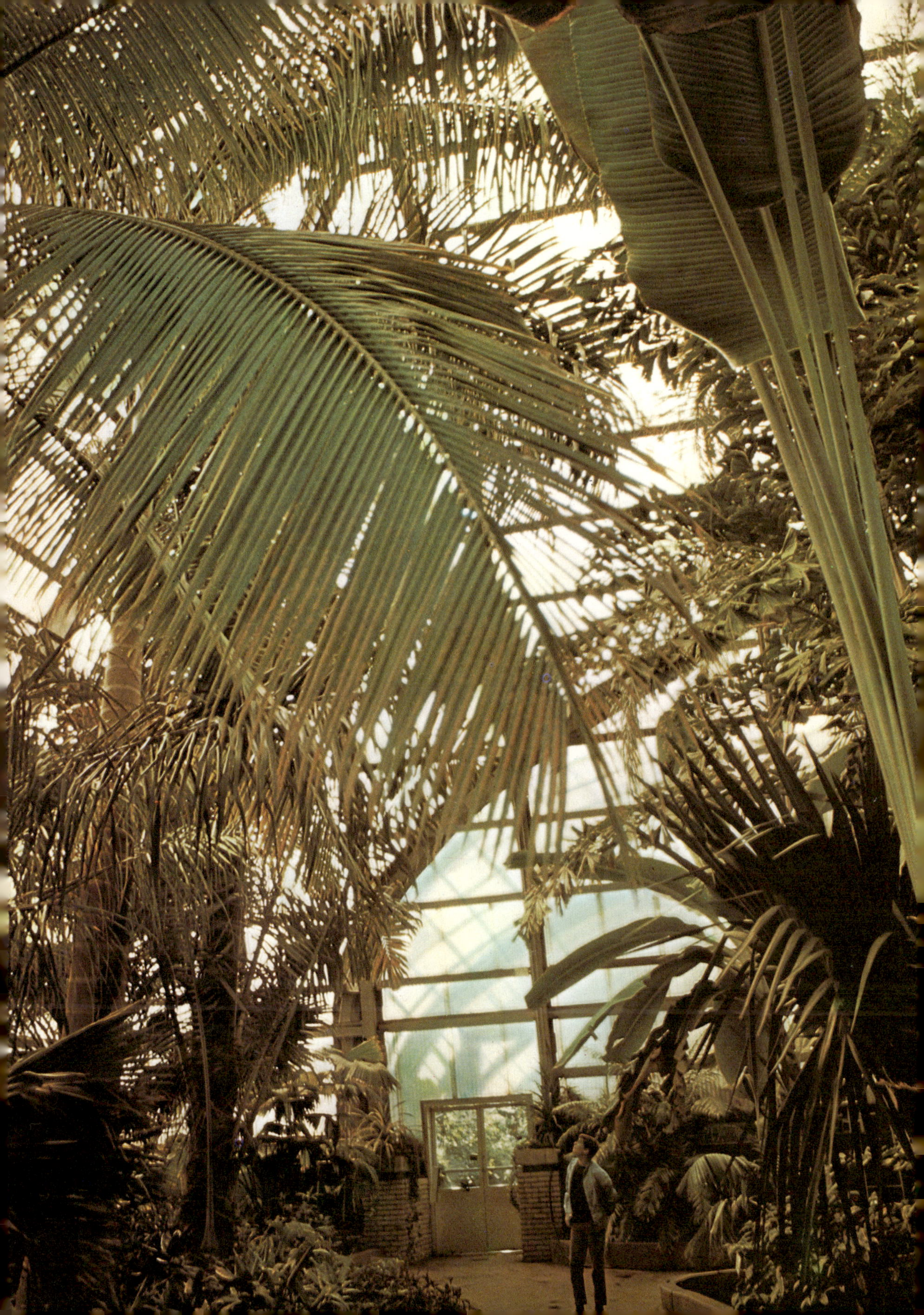

BEASTS AND GAMES FOR THE MILLIONS

More than four million persons, from toddlers to dodderers, visit the Lincoln Park Zoo during an average year, attracted not only by the usual lions, tigers, polar bears, orang-utans (one of these was born in the zoo during 1968—a rare happening), birds, reptiles and other attractions, but also by the Children's Zoo, which houses the young and newly-born animals, and the Farm, where city youngsters may gaze in wide-eyed wonder at such strange creatures as cows, horses, pigs, sheep, and other exotic beasts. In the Children's Zoo, as an added attraction, young visitors are permitted to watch while the animals are fed—many of them from bottles—and may even pet their favorites, to the mutual delight of admirer and admired.

The Chicago Park System is comprised of 438 parks with a total acreage of 6,829, offering facilities for archery, baseball, bathing, bicycling, bowling-on-the-green, riding, casting, football and soccer, golf (three nine-hole and one eighteen-hole courses), handball, boating, horseshoes, shuffleboard, swimming, tennis, running, trap-shooting, volleyball, and too many indoor activities to mention, though they do include lapidary shops, model train layouts, and a rifle range.

In a recent year almost 60 million persons visited the parks, and almost 10 million used the fifteen large and fifteen small beaches, where 372 rescues were made and there were no fatalities. Whether Chicagoans want to hear free concerts, watch a regatta, learn life-saving, attend a day camp, or watch (or take part in) amateur theatricals, the parks can satisfy them. In addition to the parks, the Chicago Park District operates seven harbors, 223 fieldhouses, Soldier Field, Adler Planetarium, Garfield Park Conservatory, the Underground Parking garages and Gately Stadium.

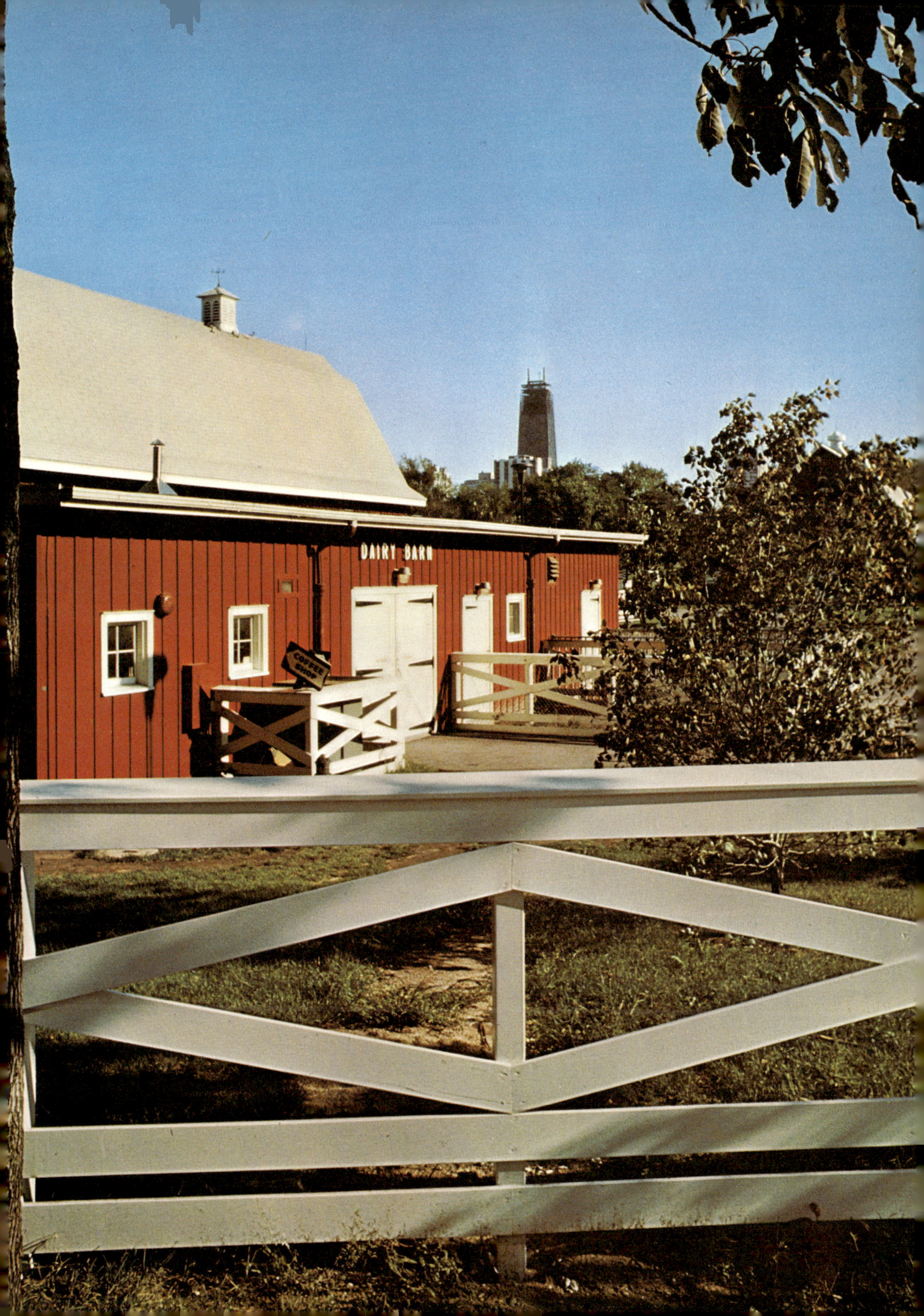
DAIRY BARN
COFFEE SHOP

AS PURE A PRODUCT AS SPRING WATER

Credit for the excellence of Chicago's drinking water, at least that portion of it consumed north of 39th Street, lies with this gigantic filtration plant, begun in 1952 and dedicated in 1966. This Central District plant occupies 61 acres, of which 10½ acres make up the Milton Lee Oliver III park, which honors the memory of Private Oliver, an eighteen-year-old Chicagoan, who earned the Medal of Honor by throwing his body on top of an enemy grenade in Vietnam. Oliver was killed, but his comrades escaped.
    The plant itself, which processes 960 million gallons of water daily, and can raise this output to 1 billion, 7 million gallons cost $105 million. A computer-operated device takes three-hundred-plus purity readings each twenty-four hours, and a fish-net 1,000 feet long and 24 feet wide keeps alewives out of the intake pipes. The tunnels bringing the water in are 20 feet in diameter and are cut into hard limestone 200 feet below the water level. Facilities at the plant include boat docks, railroad tracks, and a truck terminal, and there is closed-circuit television to monitor operations, make security and machinery checks, watch traffic control, and the mixing of chemicals.
    Little wonder that in 1964 the American Society of Civil Engineers chose the filtration plant as the year's outstanding civil engineering feat, or that the plant's final product is as pure as spring water.

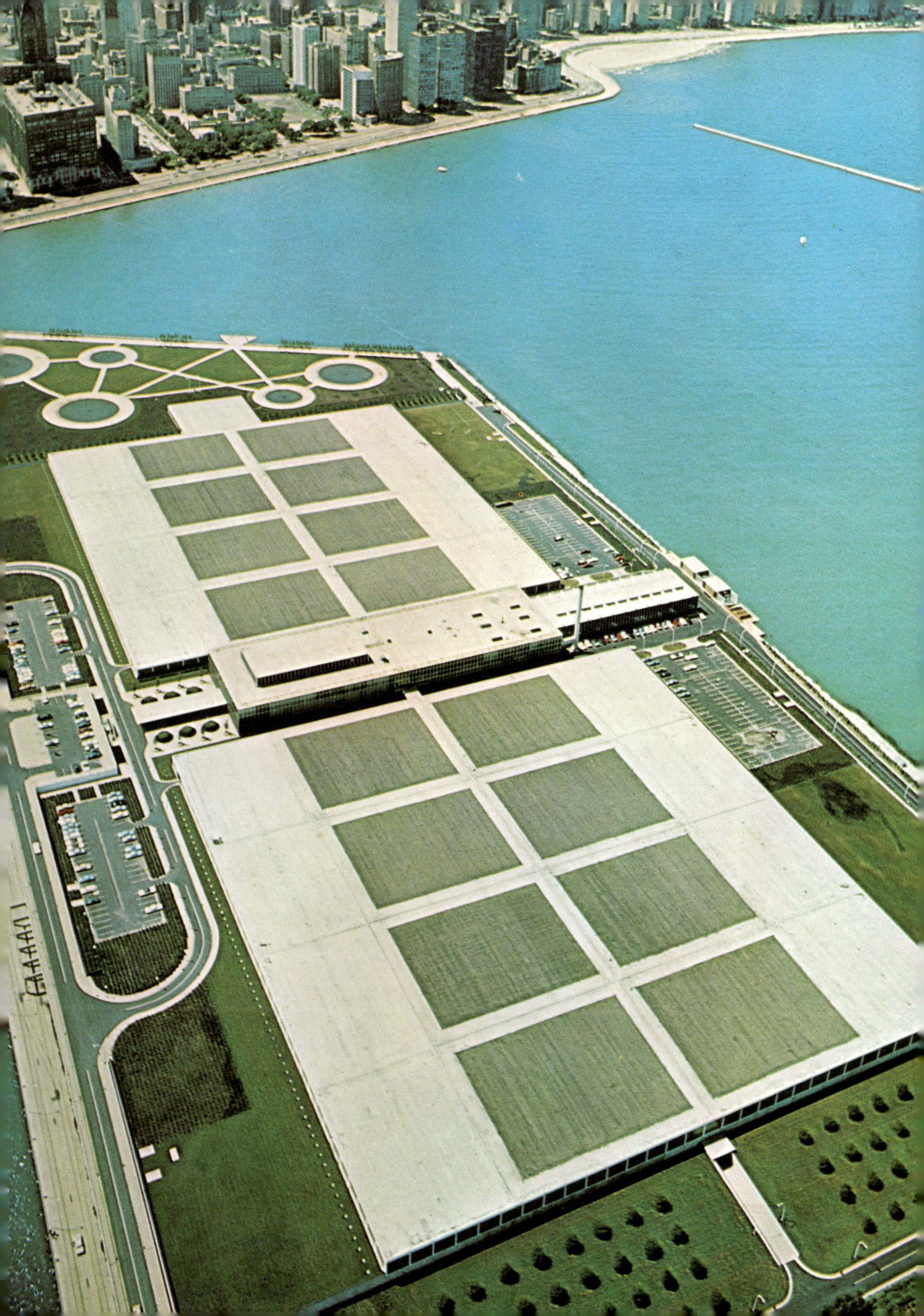

A WAY TO EXPLORE THE HEAVENS

Whether you would like to know exactly how the heavens appeared to the Three Wise Men when the Star of Bethlehem heralded the birth of Jesus, or hear a lecture explaining how man uses the sun, moon, and stars to keep a watchful eye on time, or wish simply to examine a superb collection of astrolabes, armillary spheres, celestial globes, sun dials, watches, clocks, calendars, telescopes, and other instruments used in astrology, navigation, and the study of mathematics, continue up this double roadway, past the flaming red flowers, and into the Adler Planetarium.

This three-level building, in the shape of a dodecahedron, was donated to the people of Chicago in 1930 by a local philanthropist, Max Adler, and was the first of its kind in the United States. Since that time it has become one of the most useful and fascinating of Chicago's many museums. You may drop in for the fun of it, or because you want to take a course in basic or advanced astronomy, navigation, or mirror-making.

The Theater of the Sky, which seats 450 persons (at 50 cents apiece), permits the lecturer to arrange the moon and stars as they were at any time in the world's history or even as they will be in centuries to come. The chances of finding life on other planets are discussed, as is the question of unidentified flying objects, and such phenomena as meteors, comets, eclipses, aurorae, supernovae, and halos are reproduced and explained—both scientifically and as they are regarded by the superstitious.

It might even be said—though not by me—that every show has an all-star cast.

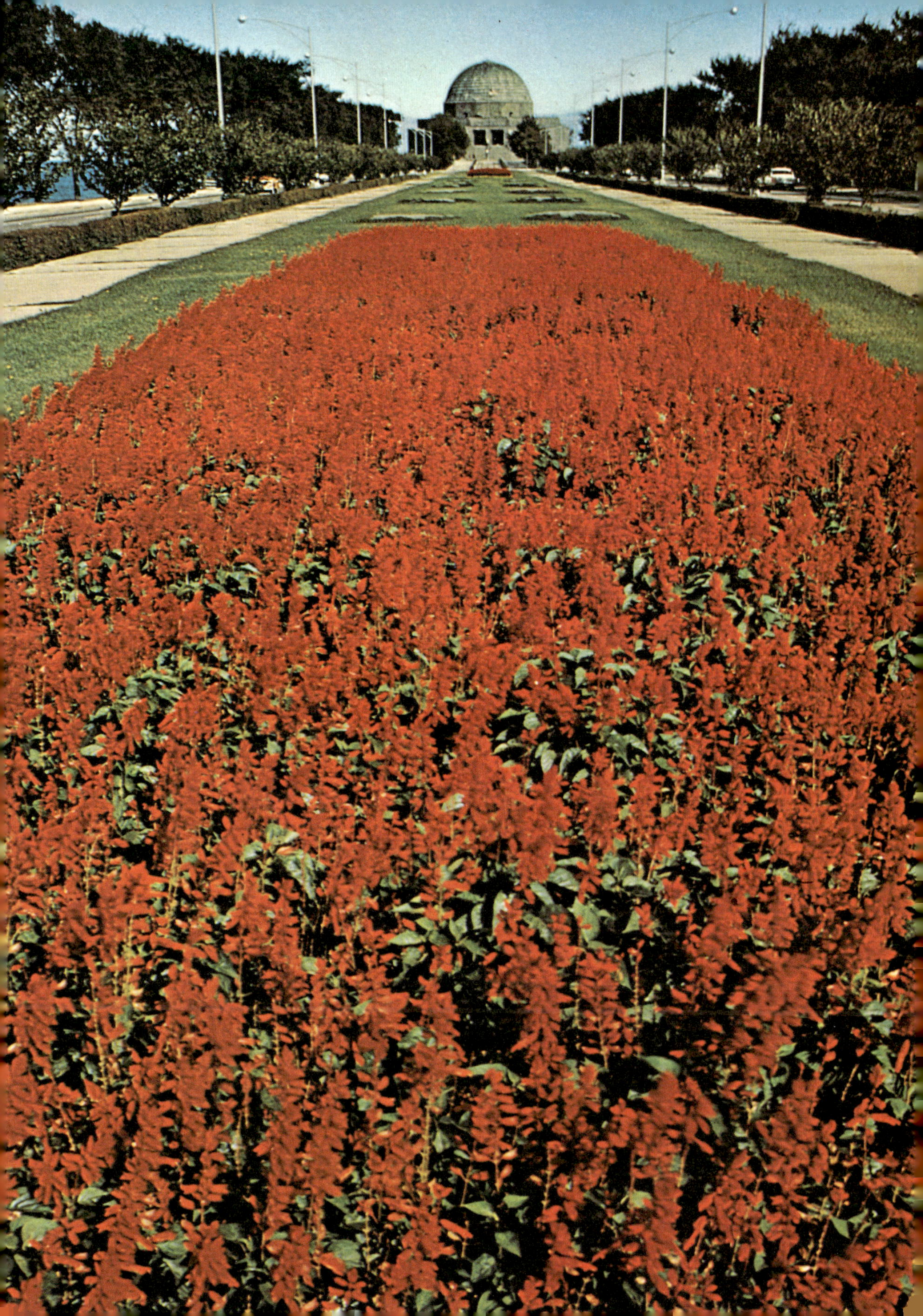

DOWN IN A COAL MINE

Museum of Science and Industry officials refer to that building, with its 14 acres of exhibits, as Chicago's number one tourist attraction—and they may be right. Each year something over three million visitors throng to 57th Street at the lake front to look at everything from the U-505, the German submarine captured intact by Admiral Dan Gallery during World War II, to the exhibit of historic aircraft, to a display of chicken eggs which hatch as you watch.

This attendance figure, as Roger Lome, who handles public relations for the Museum is happy to point out, is more than the total yearly home attendance of the Cubs, White Sox, Bears, and Black Hawks. One of the reasons for this is that the museum, which permits you to descend into a model coal mine so real that no one with claustrophobia should take the trip, also provides a great many exhibits which may be lighted, listened-to, or set in motion by the visitor himself.

Since Julius Rosenwald, the merchant-philanthropist, founded the Museum in 1926 it has become world famous. Museums in Tokyo, Cairo, and Toronto were modeled along comparable lines, and when New York and Kansas City were planning new science museums the Chicago institution again became a prototype.

I once drove an out-of-town guest to view the Science Museum after closing hours and parked close to the U-505 which, I explained had been seized by a boarding party directed by Admiral Gallery. The guest was fascinated and seemingly impressed. He glanced at a couple of historic locomotives which keep the U-boat company and asked:

"Did the admiral capture those, too?"

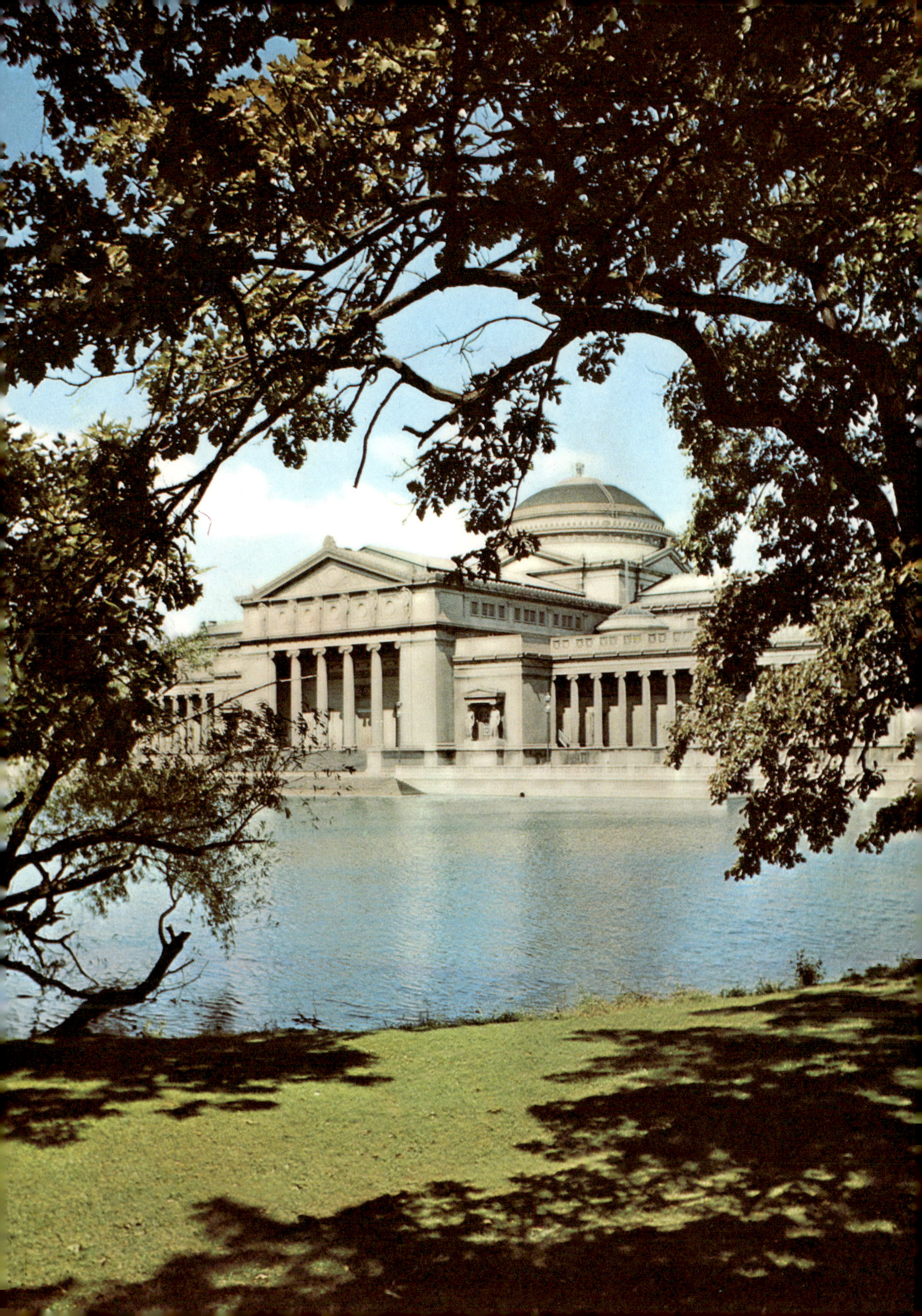

LANDMARKS IN THE LOOP

Experts on the architecture of the city will have a ball identifying all the buildings shown in this aerial shot, taken from somewhere above, and below, Wabash and Lake Avenues. It shows a portion of the Loop, looking northward along Michigan and Wabash Avenues. Just to give you a head start, the large building to the upper right or northeast, is the Prudential, at the corner of Michigan Avenue and Randolph, anti-gogglin from the Public Library. That word is one I picked up once while covering a trial in Tennessee. I know it means kitty-corner, but don't guarantee the spelling.

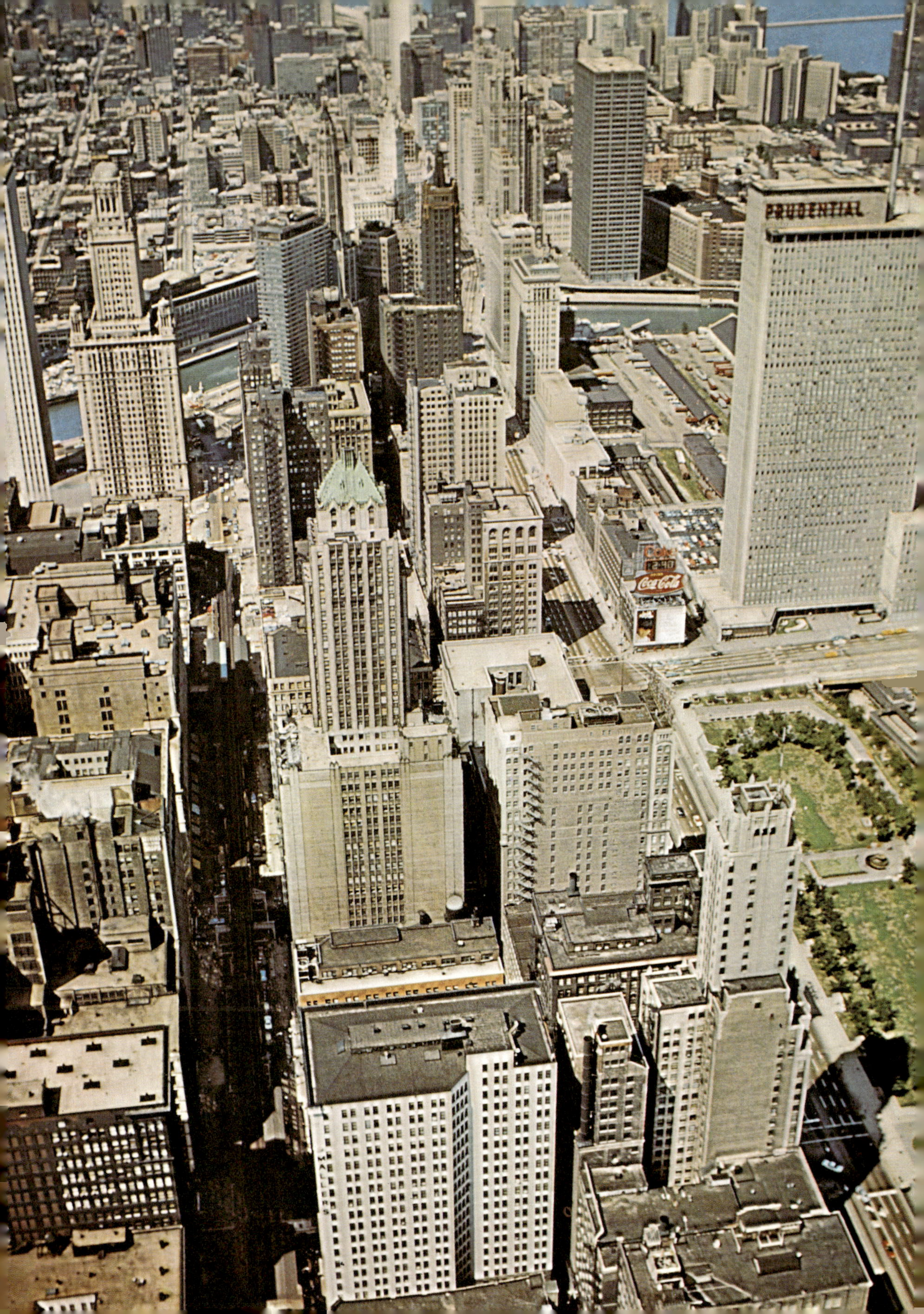
PRUDENTIAL
Coca-Cola

WHY AND WHEREFORE OF THE LOOP

One of the most typical of all Chicago sounds is the screech of elevated wheels as the cars negotiate the various turns along the right of way. Aside from the unsightly aspects of rails above the ground, supported by an ungainly steel framework, the elevated trains are a fine answer to the problem of surface travel and a faster way to go from here to there than most, at least during rush hour. You know of course that the Loop, Chicago's downtown business area, derived its name from the fact that the elevated tracks form a metal loop around that part of town. Right? Wrong!

According to a newspaper account published in the mid-forties, the elevated structure, which runs above Lake, Wells and Van Buren Streets and Wabash Avenue, went into operation in October of 1897—several years after the downtown section had become known as the Loop. The term as first used, the story says, referred to the business section enclosed by a ground-level "loop" formed by the tracks of the Chicago City Railways in the eighties. This continuous line of track was necessary to avoid the waste of time that would have been caused by changing horses from one end of the car to the other or using a turntable to accomplish the turnaround.

Instead there was "a parallelogram composed of a single track on Madison Street, Wabash Avenue, Lake Street and back to the starting point on State Street."

Sorry about that.

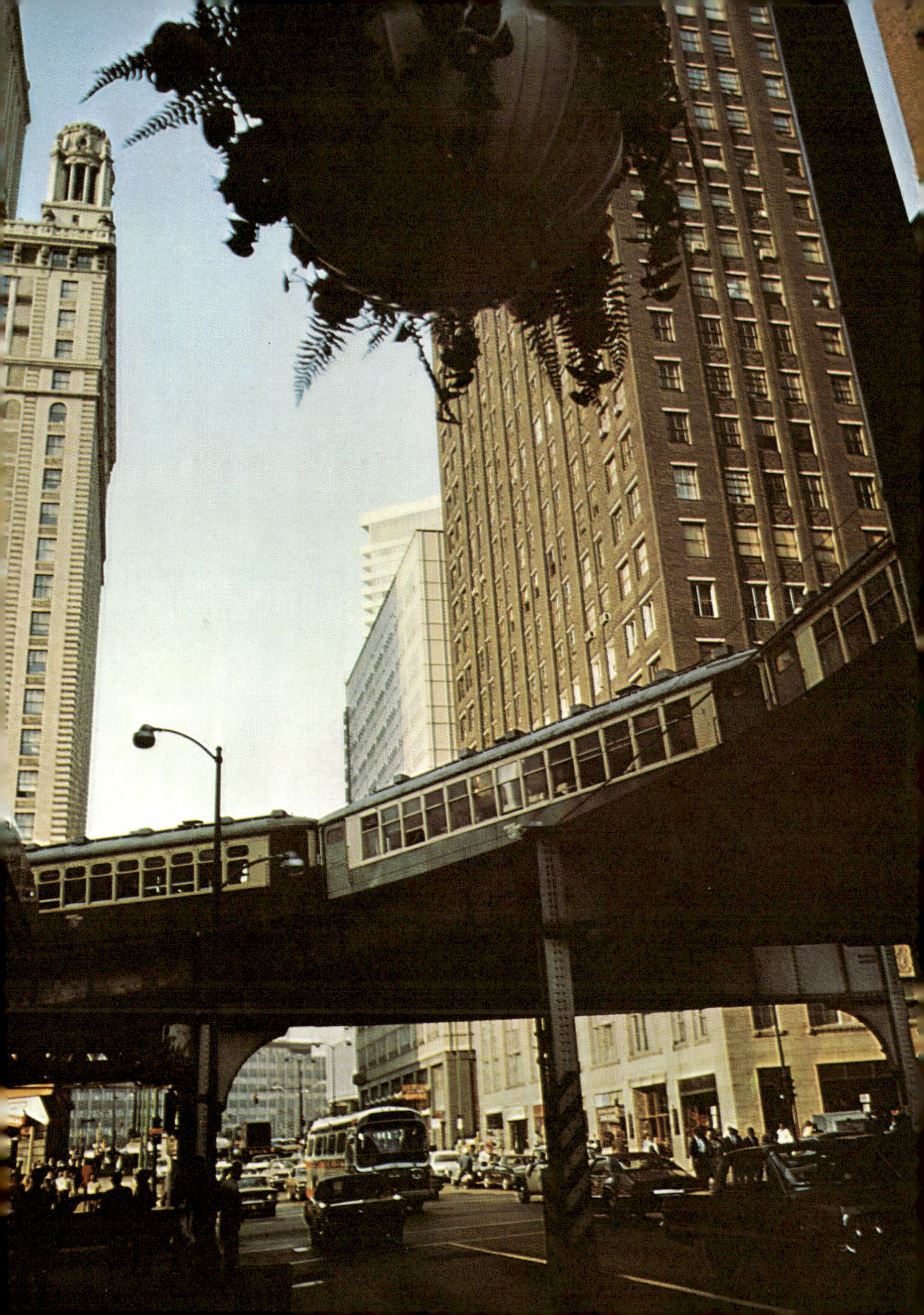

ARRIVALS AT BUSY O'HARE AIRPORT

Use of a long lens on Archie Lieberman's camera brings this cluster of United Airline planes closer together, and also pulls in the TWA and Ozark jets in the far background. But this deliberate distortion serves to create the perfect correct impression that Chicago-O'Hare International Airport, only twenty-five minutes or so from downtown except in bad weather or the rush hour, is the world's busiest civil airport with—unless the FAA has cut down the number by now—more than 1,700 flights on an average day and more than 100,000 travelers in and out on some of the days when everyone wants to be on the move at the same time. It is a common occurrence for planes to be "stacked up" overhead for varying periods during the peak arrival and departure times, and congestion on highways leading to O'Hare often is so bad that travelers unaccustomed to this delay factor miss their planes. So if you're traveling out of town by plane you would be wise to check with some knowledgeable doorman or taxi driver on the amount of time needed to make the hotel-to-airport trip, or to ask when you purchase your ticket what hour you should catch the limousine.

    Lots of people go to O'Hare just to watch the planes take off and land, an entertainment which is enhanced if you use one of the observation decks for the purpose.

TWA
N1064T
OZARK
UNITED
N7087U
BOEING 727
ITED
N902?U
BOEING 737
F52

THE EVER-CHANGING SKYLINE

This shows the western shoreline of Lake Michigan, and a portion of the city along, and adjacent to, the Outer Drive, from a point somewhere above Lincoln Park and north of that area. There is a lagoon on the right, and if you know Chicago well you will realize that a building or so is missing in the background. People were always doing that to Archie—rushing up buildings, apparently just for spite, immediately after he had finished photographing a neighborhood. He never did become really reconciled to it, but the deep melancholia which came upon him the first two or three times this happened finally lightened. Now he simply mutters, "*C'est la vie*," which seems to mean that at least they didn't empty the lake.

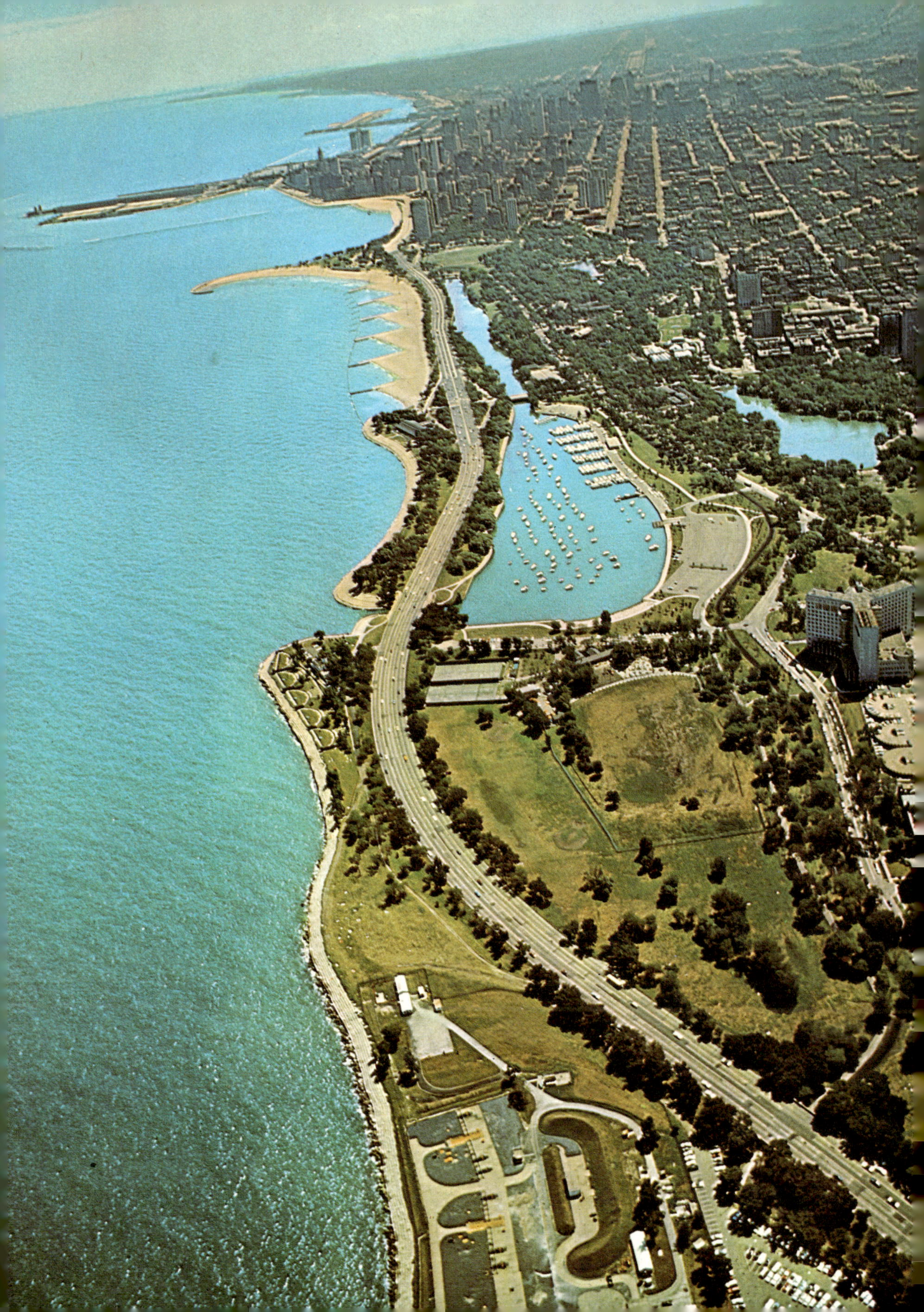

WHY AN AIR VIEW IS SUPERIOR

Here is one of the most appealing views of Chicago I have ever seen, showing as it does the meandering river, with its succession of break-in-the-middle bridges; Marina Towers, which may have been intended to be looked at from this angle; the Equitable Building, left, and the United of America Building, right, with Lake Michigan a sparkling promise in the background.

It is clear that a view of a great city from the air gives the city qualities unseen or overlooked from the ground. Its streets are now more clearly defined; its rooftops disclose unexpected symmetries. And there are disclosed oases of trees and gardens that are hidden from groundlings.

This may be an appropriate time to point out that the Chicago River, pictured below, does not empty its waters into Lake Michigan. On the contrary, it draws water from the lake when the gatekeepers permit, carries it six miles through the heart of the West Side, and eventually sends it to the Illinois, the Mississippi, and the Gulf of Mexico. That was not the way nature intended, nor the way those pioneers, Father Marquette and Louis Jolliet, found it. When Chicago was a fullgrown city, its engineers turned the river around and made it flow backward.

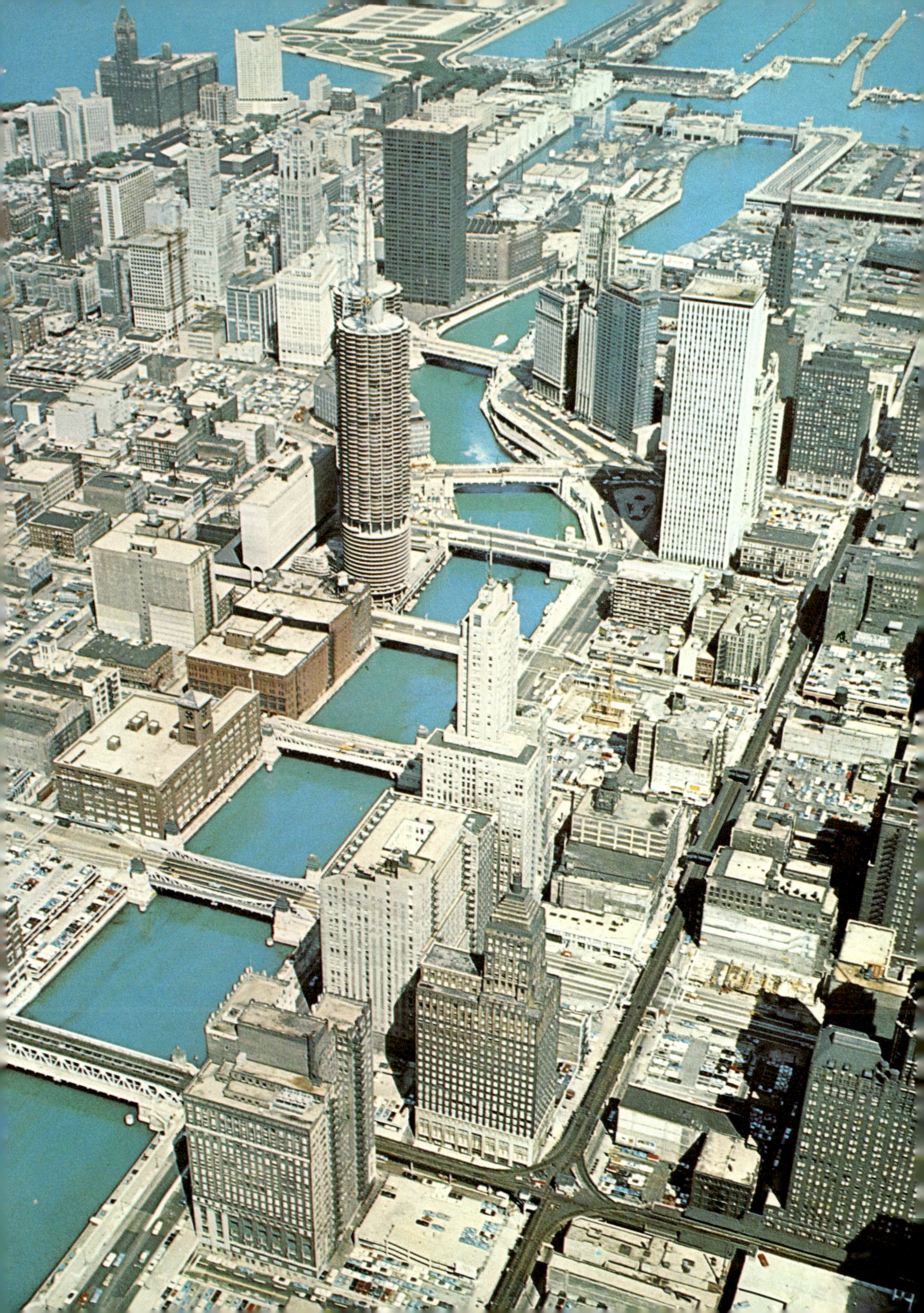

PICASSO'S TALK OF THE TOWN

Few gifts in the history of Chicago have created such wide and noisy controversy as the Pablo Picasso statue which stands in the plaza south of the Civic Center on Washington Boulevard near Dearborn Street. The Spanish sculptor himself made and gave the city the 42-inch original, on which the large steel figure (more than 50 feet high) was modeled.

When the statue was unveiled on August 15, 1967, it was received—in the words of Edward Barry, art editor of the *Tribune*, with "applause, startled exclamations, and incredulous smiles." Mayor Richard J. Daley pulled the cord that permitted the covering cloths to slide down, the Chicago Symphony Orchestra played selections from Beethoven, Bernstein, and George Gershwin, the Englewood Neighborhood Corps Youth Choir sang, and Gwendolyn Brooks, Chicago's Pulitzer prize-winning poet, read a poem for the occasion.

Few of the spectators could agree on whether the statue represented woman, bird, or dog, or how it should be rated artistically, or whether it was worth the $300,000 it cost three charitable organizations to have it made at the American Bridge Division of the United States Steel Corporation. Many liked it, many hated it, but no one who passed by could ignore the sand-colored, 162-ton figure.

One onlooker called it "not only bad, but frightening," while Alderman John Hoellen suggested that it be known as "the Chicago Buddha," and added "if you want to get junk there, get two junk automobiles that have been involved in a head-on collision on the Kennedy Expressway." Other and perhaps more knowledgeable critics lauded both statue and site and said Chicago was fortunate to own such a conversation piece.

But a North Avenue exotic dancer paid, perhaps, the most graceful tribute. She changed her name to Rusti Picasso.

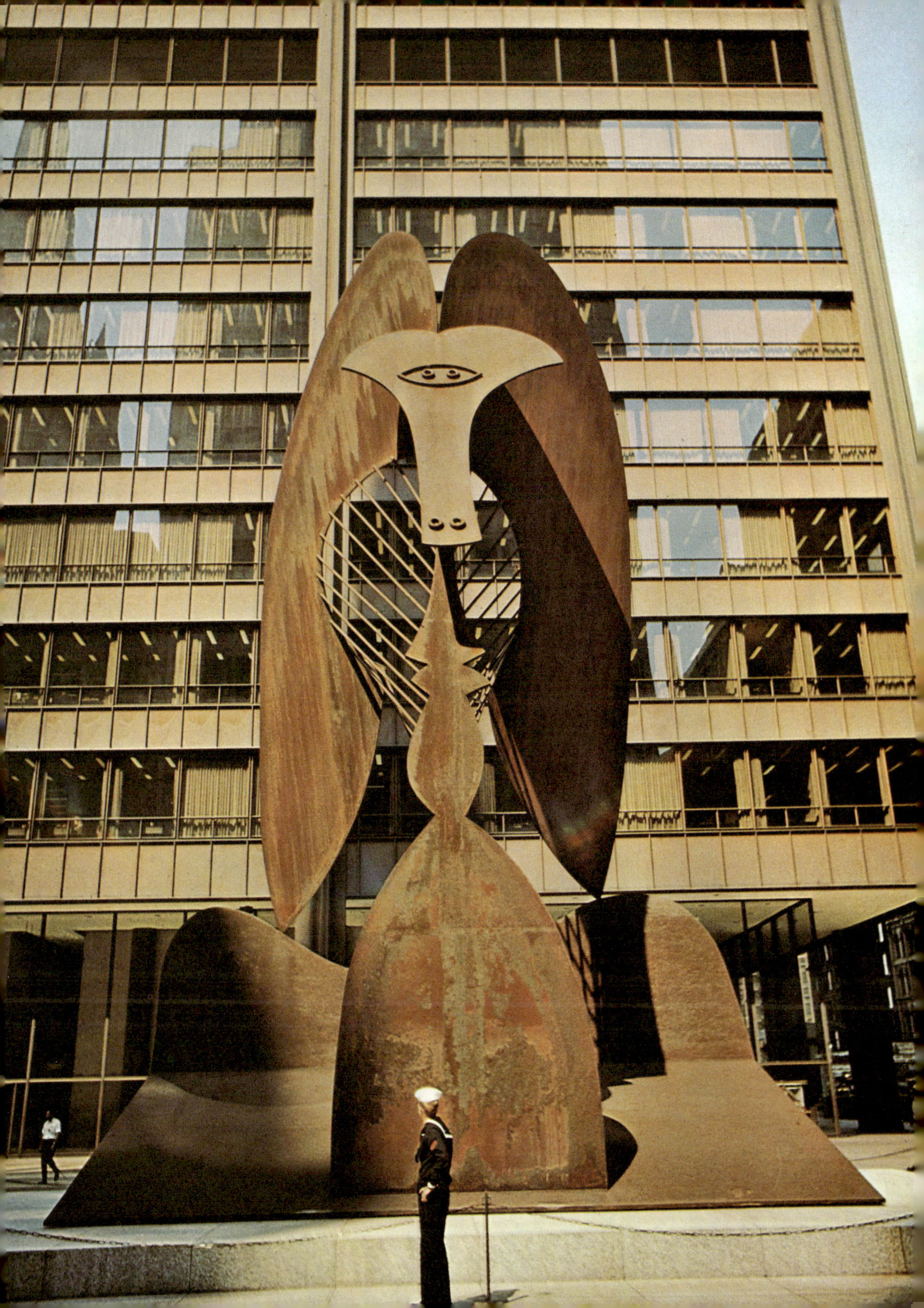

READY FOR A SUMMER SAIL

When the first warm weather comes hundreds of Chicagoans start taking their motorboats, sailboats, and yachts out of storage in preparation for another lazy summer on the water. Shown here is one of the many anchorages for pleasure craft available along the lake front. The Chicago Park District has space for more than two thousand boats of varying size, and there also are private and commercial areas. In this photograph you can see the Columbia Yacht Club, with the Prudential Building in the background. What you can't see are the happy smiles of those making ready to set out for a long day of pleasure beyond the horizon.